Scotland Road
"The Old Neighbourhood"

*The Yesteryears of Liverpool's famous
Scotland Road*

by
Terry Cooke

Cover illustration by Eric R. Monks
Cover design by Mark A. Price

First published 1987
Reprinted 2001

Published by Countyvise Limited, 14 Appin Road, Birkenhead, Wirral, Merseyside CH41 9HH
ISBN 0 907768 02 4

Copyright ©Terence Cooke, 1987
Photoset and Printed by Birkenhead Press Limited, 14 Appin Road, Birkenhead, Wirral, Merseyside CH41 9HH

*Dedicated to the
memory of my
Mother & Father.*

Old man in Great Homer Street – near Collingwood Street, 1890.

Contents

A court off Great Homer Street near Rose Vale about 1910. Courts such as this were typical of poorer working class accommodation. For all the sixty people living in the court, the only water supply available for cooking, washing and personal cleanliness was the single communal tap in the centre of the court.

Acknowledgements

I would like to express my thanks to the many people who have assisted me during the preparation of this book. My research work was greatly assisted by the co-operation I received from the very efficient staff of the Liverpool Central Library , Local History and Records Office. They willingly procured from their archives many interesting items of information which I have included in this book. Many of the excellent photographs reproduced here are part of the large collection of photographs retained in the Central Library. For allowing me to use this material, I wish to thank the City Librarian.

In order to establish authentic historical details, many books and articles were consulted. In addition, numerous archive copies of the 'Liverpool Daily Post & Echo' were examined, and found to be a valuable source of accurate background information. Among the references consulted were:— 'Memorials of Liverpool (Picton); 'Catholic History of Liverpool' (Burke); 'Charitable Effort in Liverpool' (M. Simey); 'Daily Post' 7th November 1883; 'Liverpool Review' 17th November 1883; 'Liverpool Review' 10th August 1887.

I greatly acknowledge the help given to me by Ken Stanton of the League of Welldoers, who provided some valuable historical information, and kindly permitted me to reproduce many interesting photographs from the archives of the League of Welldoers.

For kind permission to reproduce copyright material, acknowledgements are made to the 'Liverpool Echo'. For permission to use photographs from the City Engineers Department, I am grateful to the City Engineer, Liverpool City Council.

I am grateful to George Burns for allowing me to use his sketches and photographs; L. Wardell and D. Knight (Merseyside Police) for the use of their sketches; 'Scottie Press' who provided many first class photographs; Chris Dunleavy; Frank Roberts; Mrs. Wall (St. Anthony's); Mrs. M. Singleton; John Harrison; Mrs. B. Downes and Mrs. D. Knibb all of whom allowed me to utilise their material.

I acknowledge the assistance I received from the many people who had lived in the Scotland Road and Great Homer Street district, and who were prepared to talk to me about their experiences in the area. In many cases these people were able to speak, either from their own personal experience, or as a consequence of heir parents involvement and account of events which had taken place.

I would like to thank Pat and John Emmerson for giving me the benefit of their professional guidance and assistance.

In earlier editions of this book photographs which were the copyright of Arthur Johnson were inadvertently incorrectly credited. We are pleased to acknowledge that photographs on pages 13, 14, 15, 35, 36, 38, 45, 58 and 94 were taken by Mr Arthur Johnson and we gratefully acknowledge his permission to use them.

Finally, I wish to thank my wife and family for their help and encouragement.

Publisher's Dedication

Terry refers to the help he received from Pat Emmerson. Unfortunately, Pat died at a tragically young age during the preparation of this book. Born and brought up in Liverpool, Pat was fully committed to the concept of publishing books about this area and worked extremely hard on this book and others. We place on record our debt to her and publish this book as a tribute to her.

Preface

The heyday of world famous Scotland Road is recalled in this account, written by a born and bred 'Scottie Roader'. Memories go back to the days of cobbled streets and barefooted urchins, Paddy's Market and Mary Ellens. There are happy, heartwarming, and heartbreaking stories, all with the ingredient of nostalgia about them. Memories of people who have known the narrow back alleys through war and peace, and shared triumphs and tragedies.

Reproduced in this account are pictures of life in the close knit community of Great Homer Street and Scotland Road during the 1890's and early 1900's. It is not a complete history of the area, but rather it attempts to evoke some fond memories of the past, which many people hold dear to their hearts.

There have been many changes in the area since 1930, and it is difficult even for those people who have lived through it, to appreciate just how dramatic the changes have been to our way of life. For example, in those days we would stop in the street and excitedly point to the spectacle of an aeroplane flying in the sky, today we stop and watch as a horse canters by.

Reliable information has been collated about life in the early days of this world famous road. This account will be of tremendous value to future historians of the area. An interesting document of facts which will be welcomed by both past and present residents. It will be of particular interest to the many exiled 'Scottie Roaders' throughout the world, many of whom will reflect on a youth spent in the warmth of a great friendly community. What days they were, those days of long ago!

Byrom Street 1910, memories of a childhood spent in a great friendly community. In this picture we see the Public House Grapes Inn, Banners the Chemist, Millicans Tobacconist, Dixons Cocoa Rooms, and Burrows General Store. The Church is St. Stephens which stood between Byrom Terrace and Cartwright Place.

The rows of tiny cobbled streets running down to the river – this was the heart of Liverpool.

Introduction

In the 1950's Scotland Road was earmarked to become a giant motorway. To enable this to happen, the heart was savagely torn out of this close knit community. Scotland Road was slaughtered, the pubs, schools, churches, shops, cinemas, business premises, and the cosy little back to back houses in the cobbled streets were ruthlessly bulldozed to heaps of rubble. With its inhabitants scattered by slum clearance to the outskirts of the city, Scotland Road to-day remains only a story — a fascinating story to be related by parents to their children. The people were uprooted from the homely atmosphere in which they were born, and moved to unfamiliar surroundings in which they felt lost and lonely. Some old people were reluctant to move very far away, and were allocated accommodation on the hillside towards Everton, in high rise flats and maisonettes. There were many people however, who were forced to break away completely from the area; for these people, the move was heartbreaking. The bulldozers completed the rape of Scotland Road; the road which for so long was the heart of the city, was now dead, a victim of what the planners referred to as progress — a programme which created destruction, where once there existed a warm community life.

The council's programme provided for the construction of concrete ghettos and streets in the sky on the new housing estates. This was all part of the planners' project for Scotland Road to become a multi-lane highway, with plantations of trees, and a landscape approach to the second Mersey Tunnel. The destruction of the family communities of Great Homer Street and Scotland Road, resulted in terrible loneliness for some people, particularly those who lived alone. These people had been moved to a strange environment in which they were unhappy, and in which they missed the traditional caring spirit that had been so typical of the residents of their old neighbourhood, people they had known all their lives, and who cared about each other.

People having spent all their lives in the area, were very unwilling to uproot themselves and move to unfamiliar places on the outskirts of the city. A typical example of the upheaval suffered by residents, was the case of the lady who lived in Newsham Street and had worked in the old Rotunda Theatre. She had been born in the street and had lived there for fifty seven years. Her schooldays (and her mother's) had been spent at St. Anthony's School, and in later years, all her five children (now married) also attended the school, which was situated just across the cobbled street from where they lived. They were all very content in their own cosy little home, which held many wonderful memories for them. When the Housing Department officially informed her that her home was to be demolished, and that she was to be offered alternative accommodation in a high rise flat on a housing estate, she was very sad. Her entire life had been centred around the Great Homer Street area, all her relatives and friends were there. She remembered with affection, all the happy times they had experienced in the area over the years. The very happy schooldays at St Anthony's, the wonderful street parties for the children, the Christmas and New Year celebrations every year in 'Newsham House' — the local pub on the street corner. There had been so many happy times, such reliable neighbours, all this would be gone forever. She was so unhappy, and very reluctant to move. But in spite of this she was eventually compelled to accept accommodation in a multi-story council flat in Kirkby. When she first moved, she missed her old surroundings so much, that she fretted, lost weight and became ill. She would sit alone in her new home crying, she was very depressed and longed for the place where she was born, the place where all her happy memories were. Sadly, this was not be be, for soon all the houses in Newsham Street were demolished, the school, the stables, the blacksmiths all gone.

Back to back houses – Conway Street.

The ties of Scotland Road were very strong; some women who had moved to the new estates returned three times each week to what was left of Great Homer Street. Each Saturday they would arrive early to do their shopping in the market in the morning, and in the afternoon they would visit relatives and lifelong friends who were living in the area. On Sundays, the meh who had moved out with their families, returned to the pubs to enjoy a pint with their mates. Some of these people had remained close friends from their schooldays many years before.

In more nostalgic moments, we all spend some time thinking of bygone days, reflecting on days in which we appeared to live a more orderly way of life. Family life and respectability was very apparent in those days. To-day there appears to have been a complete break down of the family unit, the same family unit which came through two world wars, including the terrible May blitz of 1941.

There were hard times in the past, cruelly hard for some, days without the modern luxuries of television, hi-fi's, fridges, cars, washing machines, video's and the like. Yet they were days in which elderly people were quite safe in their homes at night, not being afraid to open their front doors after dark; in fact, front doors in these little streets were never closed. Those were the days when you could leave a bicycle outside a shop, knowing that it would be there when you came out.

Scotland Road was more a way of life than a working class area of Liverpool. It produced a rather special kind of 'Scouse' who was both tough and kind hearted. All the world was aware of the traditional toughness, but only those who lived in the area were aware of the extent of their kindness. In Scottie Road you could never be ill and alone. At the first indication of sickness or domestic problems of any kind, the friendly neighbours would be there to help, and to share what little they had. For the people who knew and loved 'Old Scottie Road' nothing could ever replace it. They have memories of hard times, of which there were many, and of more happier times, and there were many of these too. The past always appears more attractive than the present. Whenever friends gather and talk about the past, the conversation invariably turns to the 'good times we had'. Maybe this is because these days have been lived, and the heartaches and challenges have been met and overcome. The proud spirit of 'Scottie Road' will live on, the stories and the characters have remained for years. The famous battle hymns and ballads that belong only to the area, will always be remembered.

In this tale of Scotland Road, we meet many of its colourful characters, and relive some of its great moments. It would of course be impossible to record all the developments over the years, but we can try to stop time still for a moment here and there, to attempt to capture the feeling of the people, and the atmosphere of the years gone by. Hopefully at the conclusion of this fascinating tale, you will perhaps understand why Scotland Road is famous all over the world, and why it is the kind of place, which exiled 'Scottie Roaders' get so sentimental about.

Gordon Street.

Typical cellar type house which was "home" to the people of Scotland Road.

15

Local History
Street Names & Buildings

An Act of Parliament to widen and repair the road was passed in 1771. The expected development in the area did not take place, houses were not built as quickly as had been anticipated. For many years the fields on the east side of *Scotland Road* were brickfields, in which there were many deep pits. These pits were full of water and there were often bodies found in them.

In 1796 *Rose Place* was the furthest point going north.

In 1803, great developments were taking place which took many years to complete. A new street in a direct line from the bottom of *Rose Place*, northwards to *Mile End* and opposite to *Virgil Street*. This new road was given the name *Scotland Road*.

These side streets in the area were all called after celebrated men:- *Wellington Street, Ellenboro Street, Horatio Street, Great Nelson Street, Collingwood Street.*

In 1802, Mr. Edward Houghton erected a mansion at the corner of *Great Nelson Street* and *Great Homer Street.*This was known as Squire Houghton's. Many years later a Public House was erected on the site, this was called the 'Houghton Arms'.

In 1803, *Beau Street* was the furthest point going north.

The first street to break the monotony of the rural district going north from the town was *Westmoreland Place*. It was laid out about 1804, and for many years it remained a quiet street of beautiful gardens. There were no houses beyond this point until you reached Kirkdale. It was not until 1829 that houses were built in the area.

In 1810 two notable mansions were built by a John Mather in *Great Homer Street*, one was occupied by a John Cropper. About 1857, the mansions were demolished and streets were laid out on the site. The streets were :-*Conway Street, Gordon Street,* and *Elias Street.*

There were two streets — *Seacombe Street* and *Ellison Street*, which were named after a Mr. Seacombe Ellison, who inherited some of the property of the Seacombe family in the locality.

Roscommon Street, was named after the Earl of Roscommon. The street was formed by Mr. Joshua Rose who lived in a mansion nearby, he was responsible for the development of many streets in the area.

The first houses were built in *Prince Edwin Street* in 1815, a detached house was built by Roger Adamson. In later years, the house was occupied by Mr. David Hodgson, Lord Mayor of Liverpool in 1845.

In 1828, some builders purchased a field which was situated about half way to Kirkdale on the east side of *Scotland Road.* They formed a street which they named *Bostock Street.*

Wealthy business gentlemen with offices in Dale Street, would retire each week-end to their cottages. *Collingwood Street, Virgil Street,* and *Dryden Street,* consisted of walled gardens planted with fruit trees and flowers in which nestled snug little cottages.

Situated opposite *Virgil Street* was *Mile House*, the proprietor was Kitty Eccleston who was famous for making meat pies. Many people on holiday would make a special trip out to the country to eat Kitty's pies, and spend the afternoon on *Bevington Hill* and *Summer Seat*. There were beautiful gardens in the vicinity with uninterupted views of the river and the Cheshire Coast. One of the finest gardens in the area was that of a Mr. Gildart, people would visit his gardens and summerhouse. Many years later the area was developed and houses constructed, it then became known as *Gildarts Gardens*.

Limekiln Lane was originally named *Book Lane*. When the Lime Works was erected the name was changed.

The first council built dwellings were in fact flats erected in *Silvester Street* in 1869, the flats were named St. Martins Cottages, they consisted of four, four storey blocks of flats. There were no bathrooms, and the toilets were communal.

Lawrence Gardens, a tenement block of flats erected in 1931 at the back of *Cazneau Street.*

Before 1800, people living in the area, would enjoy a pleasant Sunday afternoon stroll from *Richmond Row* along the picturesque *Sandy Lane* to the Everton hillside.

Fontenoy Gardens, built in 1935, housed people from *Johnson Street* and *Standish Street*.

Victoria Square (Workingmens Dwellings) was erected in 1935.

Juvenal Buildings was erected in 1890.

In 1803, Liverpool itself ended where Scotland Road began, at *Sickmans Lane* or *Deadmans Lane (Addison Street)*. During the terrible plague of 1651 there was a cemetery on the site in which 200 victims were buried.

Eldon Street — Dwellings were erected in 1935.

Gerard Gardens erected 1935.

Lord Derby owned a vast area of land in *Scotland Road*, and as the area developed he laid out a number of streets. In 1856 his agent a Mr. William Moult, was very involved in the many business transactions which took place. In 1860 a street was formed on the east side of *Scotland Road*, this was named *William Moult Street.*

Howe Street was laid out to run from *Great Homer Street* up to *Netherfield Road*. It was named after Admiral Howe.

In 1829, *Great Homer Street* extended only to *Rose Vale*. There were many mansions on the Everton hillside at this time. In the afternoon and evening sun the view was very pleasing. The entire hillside was a range of cornfields and pastures. When the sunlight was reflected from the windows of the mansions on the hills, it gave the impression of a brilliant illumination.

Boundary Street was formed in 1830, it was the division between Kirkdale and Liverpool. It remained unfinished and surrounded by brick fields.

Dryden Street was for many years the northern limit of this part of the town. Up to 1830 the entire district beyond this point on both sides of *Scotland Road*, were open fields which extended to *Vauxhall Road* in the west, and Everton in the east.

Bustling Scotland Road, near Dryden Street 1908. A particularly interesting picture showing many of the typical features of the road at that time.

In 1830 building operations were commenced a little way beyond Mile End. Many streets were laid out and houses erected, the streets were named:- *Tenterden Street, St. Martin Street, Blenheim Street,* and *Woodstock Street.*

The triangular piece of land at the intersection of *Great Homer Street* and *Kirkdale Road,* was developed at various times between 1832 and 1862. The area of Kirkdale, eastwards from *Great Homer Street* up to *Netherfield Road,* remained open fields up to 1862, after which time the area was covered with a dense mass of side streets and houses.

Great Homer Street was named after a Greek poet, and there were some other streets which derived their names from Grecian times i.e. *Zante Street, Crete Street, Candia Street, Mitylene Street.*

Cazneu Street was projected by a Mr. B.B. Cazneu who lived in a large house in *Islington.*

From 1836 the erection of buildings on both sides of *Scotland Road* set in with considerable intensity. All the land between *Dryden Street* and *St. Anthony's Church* belonged to the Earl of Derby, who now began to form streets. The streets were named:- *Wilbraham Street, Penrhyn Street, Leyster Street.*

The *Church of St. Matthew* was the next building erected on the corner of *Wilbraham Street,* this building was later to become the Derby Cinema.

North Hay Market, the wholesale market for hay, straw, provender and vegetables in Great Homer Street, between *Great Nelson Street* and *Juvenal Street* opened in July 1866. It was open for the sale of vegetables in the early morning, and for hay, straw and provender during the later hours of the day. The area was also used as a parade ground for the Volunteers, there was enough space for a battalion of soldiers to manoeuvre under the market sheds.

Rose Place, Rose Vale, Rose Hill, these streets were named after a Mr. Joshua Rose, he also gave the names of poets to some of the streets in the area:- *Ben Johnson Street, Chaucer Street, Chaucer House, Virgil Street, Dryden Street, Milton Street, Addison Street, Juvenal Street, Alexander Pope Street.*

Once there were windmills and cornfields in Scotland Road which stretched down to the river. Eventually rough cobbled roads were laid through the green fields to accommodate the farm carts and horses and coaches.

The Port of Liverpool was growing fast, and ships filled the river bringing cargoes from all over the world. Docks were built on the riverside, warehouses and other buildings connected with shipping were also erected. There were many gin palaces and taverns built in the side streets.

When the sailing ships, and in later years, the coal burning vessels docked in Liverpool, hordes of seamen, all determined to have a wild spree ashore, made for Scotland Road. The pubs and drinking dens in the side streets were packed all day and night with the men from the ships, there were many different nationalities. The sailors roamed the streets in groups, at night they would seek the pleasures of the Maggie Mays in the gin palaces and drinking dens, there was one in almost every back alley between Great Howard Street and Great Homer Street, they were always packed and noisy.

Roscommon Street's claim to fame, Sir Herbert Morton Stanley, "finder" of Dr. Livingstone, lived at No. 22 Roscommon Street.

Living Conditions
Slums & Poverty

Great Crosshall Street – 1930.
The old fashioned mangle (washing machine) and tin bath can be seen on the bottom left of the picture. Possibly these belonged to one of the women who had to "take in washing" in order to feed her family.

Great Homer Street and Scotland Road has traditionally been a rough area. This reputation has remained since the time many Irish immigrants settled in the district during the potato famine. Between January and April 1847, 130,000 people swarmed into Liverpool from Dublin, Cork and other ports in a desperate attempt to escape the terrible famine in Ireland. As many as 1,500 passengers each day were landing from the packets from Dublin. Thousands of men, women and children were sleeping rough in warehouses and under bridges. Subsequently, many thousands of these people sailed to America but there were some 60,000 who remained in Liverpool, many of them in the Scotland Road area. These people faced poverty inconceivable in England to-day. At that time the city was already recognised as the worst in the country for ill health and malnutrition. The city struggled to overcome the worst crisis in its history.

There were many thousands of cellars which the authorities had already condemned as unfit for habitation. These were brought back into use to house the crowds of people; they were sleeping crowded on floors, there was no sanitation. In some of the houses in Scotland Road and Vauxhall Road there were sometimes fifty people crowded into four rooms. In one particular instance in Great Homer Street there were thirty people sleeping on the floor of one damp cellar. At this time the terrible cholera epidemic swept through Liverpool and the people crammed in these insanitary conditions were dying in thousands. The death toll reached terrible proportions; some ships anchored in the river were used as hospitals.

Still the emigrants from Ireland continued to arrive in Scotland Road but their dreams were doomed to despair. The area crammed, lack of employment, poverty and starvation was the lot of nearly all. Soon the area became a vast

19

sprawling slum, and many poor souls living there were victims of malnutrition and the cholera epidemic.

People suffered real hardship, some families had no income at all. In 1842, a survey was conducted in an effort to measure the extent of the problem. Out of 4,387 families living in the area the survey revealed that:-

1342 Families had no visible means of support.
 310 Families had an income less than 5/- (25p) per week.
 845 Families had an income between 5/- and 10/- (25p — 50p) per week.
 610 Families had an income between 10/- and 15/- (50p — 75p) per week.
 727 Families had an income between 15/- and £1 (75p — £1) per week.
 512 Families had an income between £1 and £1.10/- (£1 — £1.50) per week.
  41 Families had an income between £1.10/- and £2 (£1.50 — £2.00) per week.

Of the dwellings in which the families lived, the survey described the living conditions as follows:-

 581 Families were living in comfortable conditions.
1355 Families were living in tolerable conditions.
 764 Families were living in bad conditions.
 680 Families were living in miserable conditions.
 217 Families were destitute.

In February 1855, during the Crimean War, the people of Scotland Road suffered a terrible winter. The frost was so severe that the River Mersey was frozen over. Hundreds of residents surged each day to the parish relief offices for the meagre rations of coal and bread. There were many who died from the intense cold and lack of food. The poor desperate people could tolerate the conditions no longer, and eventually they took to the streets and rioted and looted. They broke into any shop or warehouse in which they could lay hands on food. The Army was called in to maintain order, many people were arrested and subsequently jail sentences were imposed upon them.

A court off Boundary Street 1897.

Workmens dwellings. Prince Edwin Street 1924.

Poverty in the area remained worse than anywhere in the country. Many people were living three families in a single room, there was not even a curtain to separate them. Conditions were at their most appalling in the numerous courts which were the main feature of accommodation for the poorer working class. A court was an area of about thirty feet wide on which had been erected two rows of three storey houses. Each dwelling had an area of only ten square feet, this encompassed the frontage and depth of the house. The ends of the courts were usually blocked off by warehouses which meant that access in and out of the courts was via a dark musty narrow passageway. In 1848 it was estimated that 33% of the population lived in courts, many of them without sanitation. Conditions were unbearable, with cholera and typhoid a constant threat. There were often as many as sixty people living in a single court. All these people had to use one water tap which was located in the middle of the court and a communal toilet which was at the end of the court. Because of the cul de sac formation of the courts there was no movement of air, and the atmosphere became stale, unpleasant and fusty. These dwellings continued to be over-crowded in the working class districts and the cellars in the cobbled streets remained homes of the poorest people.

In 1868 the authorities could no longer ignore the overcrowded conditions and made some attempts to deal with the problem. St. Martins Cottages was erected at the bottom of Silvester Street and Vauxhall Road. The building, a gaunt four storey block of flats, was to be one of the earliest council housing projects. The conditions in the dwellings, compared with present day standards, were grim but not when they were compared to the ghastly living conditions which existed in the back alleys and courts in the area at that time. The introduction of new bye-laws enabled efforts to be made to close some of the worst cellar slums. In 1864 the corporation had the power to demolish insanitary houses but there was no positive action taken until the 1880's; at this time there was a public outcry over slum conditions.

Some improvements were made to living conditions in 1889, when Liverpool Gas Company introduced prepayment gas meters to some fifty dwellings in Cazneau Street. This development pioneered the installation of gas in the homes of the lower income groups. But, nevertheless, conditions in the area were wretched and, as the years passed, there appeared to be no let up to the heartbreaks that these people had to face. In 1900 in Tatlock Street, there was an example of the difficulties to be overcome. The house consisted of only one living room with a gas ring for cooking on, there was a tiny back yard with a cold water tap. The woman lived there with her unemployed husband and ten children. For this unfortunate family life was a continual struggle to survive each day.

The effects of extreme poverty coupled with excessive drinking were the subject of an article in the Liverpool Review in November 1883:-

'There had been a number of houses inspected in different courts. In one we found a man lying helplessly and speechlessly drunk on a bed of sacks in the parlour. With him was a young woman in a condition of raging delirium. On the step of the house were two little children of about three and four years, clad in nothing but a shirt, and trembling and afraid to enter the house. The woman was tearing around the room, and protesting that the drunken pig on the bed was her brother, her lawful brother, and the child of the same parents. This fact or fiction, whichever it might have been, possessed a fascination for the lady, for she never ceased to scream it at the top of her voice during the ten minutes we were present in the house. We found that the children were hers, and that they had no place to sleep except the bed where the drunken man was sleeping, and on which the drunken woman would fling herself when her violence had exhausted itself.'

In 1914 there were about 400 courts in Liverpool, mostly in the Great Homer Street and Scotland Road area, and although the authorities continued in their efforts to close all the condemned cellars, there were still families living in these cellars in many of the side streets on the east side of Great Homer Street in 1940.

By 1910, generations of Scotland Road residents had suffered continual deprivation, having had to accept the unpleasantries of bad housing, lack of education, and poor medical facilities. With poverty and unemployment an ever present problem, there never was sufficient money to feed the family. Poor people struggled year after year through conditions which had become the normal way of life for the district. There was very little opportunity for the people to improve their standard of living and these desperate people had to be tough to survive the depressing conditions. This was an area where tough people lived tough lives. If you could survive in Scotland Road you could survive any where. It was no accident that years later, during the two world wars, units drawn largely from this area discharged their duties with so much distinction. These people were brave and proud, they were also humorous, always ready to laugh at life, even under the most difficult conditions.

Families were very grateful for the gifts of food which was distributed from Limekiln Lane.

Given to some of the many 'homeless' souls which wandered the streets. This entitled these unfortunate people to a 'nights lodging'.

A poor family on the doorstep of their home in Gerard Street 1890.

Children
Deprivation

Throughout the difficult times in Scotland Road no one suffered more than the street children who were subject to very harsh treatment. In Liverpool, between 1835-39, 53 out of every 100 children born, died before they were 3 years old. The infant mortality rate for England for the period 1882-1890, was about 140 per 1,000. In the Scotland Road/Vauxhall Road area in 1891, it was 264. Medical experts attributed this excessive mortality rate to overcrowded conditions, bad ventilation, inadequate warm clothing, and sometimes violence, which arose from the parents' drunkeness. In spite of the high juvenile death rate, families were usually large, family ties were very strong; there was always a special relationship between mothers and daughters.

Even when a child survived the earliest years, he or she had to struggle through a deprived childhood in the back streets and alleyways. Children were always on the streets trying to earn sufficient to live by selling oddments and begging for the price of a loaf. In 1882 their were ragamuffin children everywhere; all from impoverished backgrounds, barefoot and bedraggled, they wished only for parents of their own. Footwear was a luxury not many children enjoyed and very often they went days without food. The extent of the poverty which existed at this time is reflected in the photographs of children, bare foot and in tattered clothing. There were many of these poor souls, who would sit cold and hungry, huddled together to keep warm, in doorways of shops and warehouses. It was situations such as this which caused the first branch in Britain of the Society For the Prevention of Cruelty to Children to be formed in Liverpool in 1883.

Youngsters discovered a variety of ways of earning money. Many of the boys helped in the markets; some carried passengers bags at the Pier Head and at the Railway Stations, others earned a living as shoeblacks. Some young girls helped their mothers in the market, other less fortunate girls had to trade in the streets selling matches. There were large numbers of girls who sold bundles of wood. An account of a group of girls chopping wood in Hodson Street appeared in the Daily Post in November 1883:-

'The courts in Hodson Street seem largely inhabited by young girls who earn a precarious living by selling chips. Further down the street watercress sellers are to be found. On the day we visited, it was very wet, and the women had been driven indoors. In one house in No.1 court – a narrow close nest, with even the passage blocked up by a door – we found a tiny room filled full of these chip girls, who sat on the floor, with a heap of wood before them, chopping away, and apparently very merry. As may be imagined, the atmosphere of the place was sickening in the extreme. These girls have different districts in the town and outskirts, often walking miles before they reach their customers. They sell their chips at the rate of a penny for a dozen bunches, often however, getting much less than this. As one girl put it, "Some people is good, some people is bad, but we 'as sell the chips anyway, and we makes about tenpence (5p) per day." There are hundreds of these young girls keeping body and soul together on tenpence a day. Rough creatures as they are, there is much that is praiseworthy in them, the temptations to which they are subjected must be very great, the prospect of release from daily drudgery very alluring.'

Children found their way into the many public houses in Great Homer Street in an effort to sell newspapers and matches. These shoeless urchins would have been a common sight in the streets about 1885. The children would gather at various points, awaiting the arrival of the newspaper carts. They would purchase as many newspapers as they could afford, then they would be on the streets in all weathers, sometimes very late at night until all their papers were sold. For some of the younger children it was very exhausting. They were described by a Mercury reporter as:- *'Little half clad children, selling newspapers on doorsteps until 10pm or 11pm, sometimes asleep in the snow trying to sell the remainder of their bundles of newspapers.'*

Liverpool through its council and particularly through its charities, made great efforts to improve conditions for the children. Many leading social reformers concerned themselves with the plight of underprivileged children; they provided homes, clothing and food. There were needy children everywhere, many of them wore clothing of a rough corduroy fabric, known as 'Police Clothing' and issued together with rough footwear once a year by the Police. Both the clothing and the clogs were specially marked to prevent them

Barefoot days. The poverty of the area is reflected in this picture of barefooted children outside a public house in 1890.

being pawned. Children and their mothers would pack the local bridewell while the shirt sleeved policemen knelt busily fitting out the children with the garments and footwear which they had provided for the poor out of their own pay.

Extracts from the Annual Report of the Liverpool Society for the Prevention of Cruelty to Children — 1883-84.

A child of seven would sleep out of doors rather than go home to a cruel father. When found the child would be swarming with vermin and almost stupefied from ill-treatment. When he was taken back to his father, the father refused to have the child, and used very violent and blasphemous language. For this desertion the father was prosecuted and sent to hard labour for 14 days. When released from prison, he fetched the boy from the workhouse and told him to go and beg for his keep.

A boy of eight habitually selling papers at 11 o'clock at night. Visitors discovered it was a case of poverty, the mother was a widow of a seaman, she was in bad health and had been left with five children to support. The ages of the children were 14, 9, 8, and the twins of 4 years, her income was only 4/- (20p) from the local parish. An application for help was made to the Seamen's Orphanage, which resulted in a grant of 20/- (£1) per month.

A little girl of nine was sent out with a starved baby of 18 months to beg in the streets. The wretched, drunken mother, deaf to all entreaties, persisted in sending the girl out to beg money for drink. The girl attempted to rob a till at a public house, she was charged before the magistrate and commited to an industrial school until she was 16 years of age.

A girl of nine, wild and uncared for, untaught and desperate, was begging at night near the Sailors Home. From this very dangerous practice she took to stealing. The girl's mother was cautioned over and over again, but to no avail. The girl continued her life of crime.

Great Homer Street 1900.
A barefooted little girl earns a "copper" reciting in a Public House near the North Hay Market. The customers all appear to be farmers.

26

Hard Times

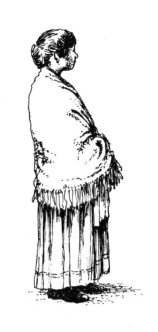

*Charitable Organisations, Dole School, Employment,
Pawnshops, Money Lenders, Medical Dispensary.*

CHARITABLE ORGANISATIONS
GAY STREET ACADEMY

In 1880, there were many charities and long established welfare organisations, which helped feed and clothe the starving people. The Gay Street Academy or 'Home of Love', provided assistance to the deprived people of Scotland Road. A journalist spent a Saturday evening in the Gay Street establishment in August 1877; this is an account of his experience, which appeared in the Liverpool Review:-

'It was within a few minutes of eight o'clock on a Saturday night last when I sought out the 'Home of Love' to see with my own eyes the character of the work with which it is occupied. The streets at that early hour were commencing to reek with Saturday night debauchery. The public houses were thronged with half-drunken people of both sexes. Ragged little urchins with bare heads and feet were flitting in and out of their doors hugging high bottles, whilst men and women staggered along the footpath, far gone in liquor. Turning into Gay Street, I stopped before some large warehouse-like doors on the left hand side of the street. It was the 'Home of Love'. From within came the tones of a piano which certainly sounded incongruous in such a locality. I entered and found myself in a long and narrow room which was well filled with a strange assemblage. They were in the full enjoyment of a Saturday night coffee supper – one of the institutions of the 'Home of Love'. At the invitation of the Rev. Herbert Wood, the clergyman in charge, I passed between the motley rows of feasters to the top of the room, where there stood a piano, and a table well decorated with flowers. Here left for a time to follow my own inclinations, I surveyed the interior of the 'Home of Love' and its Saturday night occupants. The room contained about eighty five adults, with one or two children and was well filled. The walls were coloured light blue with dark brown dado, and were profusely hung with pictures, prints and floral text cards. A huge mounted palm leaf had that evening been added to the other decorations. In the window recesses and upon the chimney piece were numerous bowls of flowers, which gave the room an appearance far different from what might have been expected in Gay Street. Flowers, I afterwards learnt, are an important adjunct in carrying on the work. They are therefore provided liberally by friends of the mission. A large illuminated banner, belonging to the Temperance Union, was displayed at one side of the platform, the other side being occupied by the piano. Mrs. Sydney Toby, one of the most staunch workers of the mission, was the accompanist for the evening. During the progress of the supper which consisted of a plentiful supply of coffee and bread, this lady played a succession of popular hymn melodies. These were evidently appreciated by the audience, to judge by the humming accompaniment which was kept up whilst the music was proceeding.

Among the people present were casual dock labourers, coal heavers, travellers, and a number of nondescripts, each of whom were in labouring garb, with the familiar neck handkerchief. There were some too, whose profession I would prefer to leave unstated, there were females present who were the poorest of the poor, there were old decrepid females bowed by the burdens of the years. All, however appeared to be happy for the moment, as they partook of the supper amid the music and cheerful surroundings.

The audience had just dispersed and the workers were about to bid each other good night, when an unexpected incident stayed their departure. A woman entered the room hurriedly and flung herself down upon her knees at one of the forms, in the attitude of prayer. The workers looked uneasily at her and each other. They knew her well. She was one of the worst characters of the Liverpool streets, and was well known to the police. She had been at the 'Home of Love' on many occasions and had always been kindly treated. She had not been rescued, though as Mr. Wood afterwards remarked to me, "We have hopes for her yet and are praying for her". Two of the ladies approached her and tried to enter into converstation with her. Without any warning she fell, or rather threw herself down full length upon the floor, convulsed in the paroxysms of a drunken fit. Those present hastened to her assistance. She dashed her head heavily and quickly against the floor, and it became necessary to hold her in order to prevent her from doing herself injury. The ladies were unflagging in their endeavors to pacify her. By kind words and attentions they

Standish Street 1890. This statue was erected in memory of Hannah May Thom, who did much charitable work for the people of this area between 1832 – 1872. The 'fountain' was a popular meeting point for generations for the residents of Holy Cross Parish.

An "alley concert" provided by Mr. Lee Jones, in a court off Kew Street in 1900; the piano and gramophone were hauled on a 'hand-truck' around the back streets of Scotland Road.

strove to calm her sufficiently to enable them to take her to her wretched home. With hair dishevelled and with eyes flashing fiercely she lay and struggled.

"Jane, Jane, gi' me a glass o' beer, gi' me a glass of beer" she shrieked.

"Nellie, Nellie, you're in the Home of Love, in the Home of Love" said one of the ladies.

"Am I in Dale Street, am I in Dale Street?, Jane gi' me a glass of beer", she shrieked again.

"Nellie, Nellie, my love don't you hear, you're in the Home of Love", said the lady again.

"Jane, Jane, I'll get seven days for this, am I in Dale Street?, God! gi' me a glass o' beer, gi' me a glass o' beer".

For about half-an-hour this continued, the little band striving to bring her round sufficiently to enable them to remove her. When the fit appeared to have passed over, they assisted her to a seat, the ladies dealing with her as kindly as they could. They treated her as though she were one of their own number, instead of a waif cast up by the sea of sin and shame. For another half an hour they attended her, speaking only loving words, but the poor drunk soddened wretch can have been conscious of little of the kindness shown to her. Midnight was drawing on apace when they deemed it safe to leave her, one of the ladies took charge of her, and saw her home. Such was my experience at the 'Home of Love' in Gay Street, Scotland Road.'

LEE JONES (LEAGUE OF WELLDOERS)

H. Lee Jones, the great Liverpool benefactor and founder of the Food and Betterment Association in 1893, will long be remembered by the City of Liverpool, whose poor and needy he helped for so many years. He continued to make tremendous contributions towards assisting the deprived families of Scotland Road, up to the time of his death in 1936. The aim of the charity was:- 'To feed, clothe, shelter and cheer, those in need, irrespective of creed'.

Vouchers like this were given to the underprivileged children in the area.

1900.
Food and Betterment Association, Limekiln Land. Barrows were loaded with containers of tea and soup, and distributed to the desperately poor people in the district.

For many years, Lee Jones organised numerous activities for the benefit of the people in the area. Concerts were arranged in the Lyric Theatre in Everton Valley and the Rotunda Theatre in Scotland Road. There were outings for groups of people to New Brighton and when they returned from their trip 'over the water' there would be a meal laid on for them at the centre in Limekiln Lane. Parties were held at Christmas time, and children from the local schools were invited. During the war years there were concerts organised to keep the children occupied; at these concerts, which were very popular in the area, there would be plenty of cocoa and cake available to the children.

In 1904 there were many charitable organisations in Liverpool, one of the main objectives was to provide meals for families who lived in poor circumstances. It was quite common in those harsh days of widespread poverty for children to have to go without breakfast. They would go to the Food and Betterment Association for their dinner and in spite of being very hungry many of the children would save perhaps a round of bread or a potato for their mothers who constantly deprived themselves of food in order that their children might eat. The cost of the meals was one halfpenny but many of the children were so poor that the meals were provided for them without payment. There was also special food for the sick.

In the depression years, in the summer weeks, the poor people of great Homer Street would be entertained by Mr. Lee Jones and some of his colleagues who would travel around the courts and alleys with a cart. They would play a portable gramophone or have a sing-song on a piano. The residents were delighted with the concerts and looked forward to them. It was one of the very few highlights of the summer for them.

Lee Jones was very involved in encouraging youngsters to participate in sporting activities. The famous Lee Jones Boxing Club was formed about 1938 and it is interesting to relate how the club was originated. One winter's night in 1938 a youngster staggered into the League of Welldoers seeking medical attention, he had suffered a knife wound during a street fight. The wound was treated in Stanley Hospital and the youngster recovered. But the incident so appalled the officers of the centre, that it prompted them to form a Boxing Club

29

in the area. It was hoped that the young men would have an opportunity to release all their aggresiveness in the boxing ring rather than in the streets. Since the club was founded many first class boxers have progressed through Lee Jones stables to become top amateur and professional fighters.

FRIENDS INSTITUTE

Although the residents of Scotland Road were mostly Roman Catholic, there was also a group of Quakers from the 'Friends Institute' in Richmond Row. In the early 1900's these benevolent people gave great assistance to the poorer people in the district particularly to the children from the dusty back streets of Scotland Road. They were taken on a day out over the water to a mansion where they were waited on by servants and butlers. The mansion belonged to shipping millionaire Sir Richard Durning Holt. The children who went on these outings will never forget those wonderful times. There were many families in Great Homer Street who were in need and were helped by the 'Friends Institute'. This little group of Quakers were very helpful and provided a tremendous amount of happiness to families in difficulties from their premises in Richmond Row. The Winstanley family managed the premises which was known locally as 'Winnys' and was financed by a tiny group of wealthy Quakers. Hot dinners and clothing were provided for the many people who went there seeking help. There were facilities provided for youngsters, which included:- billiards, table tennis, gymnasium and football, there was also a free concert every week. It is believed that the present day 'Citizens Advice Bureau' was originated by these kind Quakers in Richmond Row.

DOLE SCHOOLS

During the 1930's depression years in Scotland Road many young men in the area were unable to secure employment and were sent to what was known as the 'Dole School'. This was situated in Oldham Street, off Mount Pleasant. The attendance was for five days of the week, four hours each day. At the school they were taught a variety of useful subjects including woodwork. They were paid 7/6d (37½p) per week; this was forfeited if they failed to attend the sessions. A

The sick and the poor people of the area are visited by the 'Ladies of Charity' in Limekiln Lane 1895.

Outside the 'Food and Betterment Association', Limekiln Lane in 1900. Women queue for food, a policeman 'stands by' to maintain order.

number of 'Dole Schools' were established in other areas of Liverpool and, of course, each group formed their own football team with challenge games being played. At this time there was no hope of any type of work, and therefore it was considered by the authorities, that the introduction of the 'Dole Schools' kept the unemployed youths off the streets and out of trouble.

EMPLOYMENT

Employment opportunities had always been limited to the residents of Great Homer Street and Scotland Road. Many men from the district worked at the docks as labourers. But this work was only of a casual nature, usually on a day to day basis, with never any sort of guarantee of a regular wage packet. There was no entitlement to state benefits such as family allowances at this time and some families were so dependent on the father's meagre income that, when he was paid, the eldest boy or girl in the family would have to go down to the dock road to collect the wages from him in order to purchase food for the family for that day.

There were many young boys who decided on a sea-going career. Very often there were fathers, sons, brothers, and uncles, who went to sea as stokers or trimmers in the boiler room of one of the many old coal-burning ships that sailed in and out of Liverpool.

Young girls leaving school, went to work in bag-warehouses which manufactured sacks and bags. The buildings were very cold and damp. Besides the very bad working conditions, the wages were extremely poor.

In later years, when the employment situation improved, besides the docks or going to sea, employment for the people of the area was found in Tate & Lyle's, Silcock's, Bibby's, and Tillotson's. The girls secured work as shop assistants in town, many of them went to work in the British American Tobacco Company — the 'B.A.' as it was known to the people of the area.

PAWNSHOPS

There were pawnshops on almost every street corner in the poorer districts of Liverpool. In the deprived back streets, it was quite common for families to have to pawn some of their possessions in order to exist. But the 'Scottie Roaders' were very proud, and did not like each other to know how desperate for money they really were. In many homes the items to be pawned were collected and made up into a bundle ready to be taken to the pawnshop. The mother would discreetly peep through the window to ensure that there were no neighbours about to see the bundle — obviously destined for the pawnshop — being taken from the house. It was the usual practice to go 'the long way round' to the pawnshop, via back alleys and side streets, in order to avoid the embarrasment of meeting people you knew. Pawnshops were a thriving business in the under privileged districts. On Monday mornings long queues formed outside the pawnshops with people waiting to 'hock' their bundles of clothes, boots and shoes. If the husband was lucky enough to own a 'best suit' this would be put into

One of the many pawnshops in Great Homer Street where 'bundles' were pawned on a Monday morning and redeemed on Saturday nights.

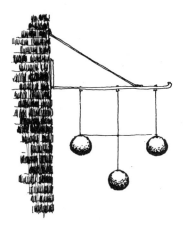

the pawnshop on Monday morning, and redeemed on Saturday night. The women came out of the pawnshop clutching their six shillings (30p) and a pawn ticket; They knew that the money they had received would enable them to provide food for the family throughout the week.

In 1900, there were numerous pawnshops in the area, among them were:—

Clarksons	234, Scotland Road,
Cooksons	375, Scotland Road,
Houghtons,	42, Scotland Road,
Newports,	337, Scotland Road,
Newports,	406, Scotland Road,
Stanleys,	186, Scotland Road,
Sturlas,	79 — 81, Scotland Road,
Fitzsimmons,	30, Scotland Road,
Bradshaws,	12, Scotland Road,
Cummins,	35, Great Homer Street,
Sturlas,	154 — 158, Great Homer Street,
Daglishs,	132, Great Homer Street,
Daglishs,	218, Great Homer Street,
Daglishs,	300, Great Homer Street,
Hasts,	175, Great Homer Street,
Berrys,	53, Richmond Row,
Healings,	175, Richmond Row,
Foxs,	34, Rose Place,
Griffiths,	110, Burlington Street,
Griffiths,	28, Titchfield Street,
Daglishs,	46, Hopwood Street,

MONEYLENDERS

In the old days in Scotland Road there were no Bank Loans available to the residents. People who required money for one reason or another had to borrow money from the local Moneylender and were charged an interest rate of 2/6d (12½p) in the pound for every week the debt remained unpaid. There was usually a Moneylender in every other street and almost all of the people had at some time needed to borrow money. Many of the Moneylenders also sold fruit and flowers from handcarts at the corners of the streets. There was one well known Moneylender who was rather a well built woman. She became intoxicated almost every Saturday night in the public houses near the North Haymarket. It usually required four policemen to arrest her and take her to Rose Hill bridewell.

MEDICAL FACILITIES – DISPENSARY

Before the introduction of the National Health Service, Doctors required a fee for providing medical attention. There were many occasions, where, because of the poor people's inability to pay for a Doctor's visit, there was no medical attention provided. In the Great Homer Street area the underprivileged children received treatment through the facilities available from what was known as the 'Dispensary' which was situated in Richmond Row. This was a gaunt Victorian building, built of red stock brick, the arches and windows having a construction of common bricks. Forboding iron railings and wrought iron gates completed the prison like appearance. Inside the building, the patients sat on rows of wooden forms which faced a line of curtained off cubicles in which the patients were examined. All manner of diseases, wounds and ailments, were treated in the 'Dispensary', which provided a much needed medical facility to the residents in the area.

From Limekiln Lane 'soup barrows' were sent out to various points on the dock road, where poor men were waiting for work. In bitter weather a bowl of soup and a slice of bread was most welcome.

Environment

Neighbours, Shops, Street Bookies, Mary Ellens,
Weddings, Confinements, Seafarers, Jiggers,
Games & Pastimes

*The Corner Shop – 'open all hours'.
This general shop was situated in the
Byrom Street area, and catered for the
needs of the neighbourhood seven days
a week.*

NEIGHBOURS

Scotland Road, in spite of its tough, bleak appearance, had an indefinable attraction which the inhabitants found endearing. There was a tremendous community spirit, a clanishness in all the little streets. This was possibly because the families lived very close together and to some degree they became family communities among themselves. They would assist each other through the many difficult situations which confronted them. They would share their last few shillings with each other. Neighbours were aware of problems which required their attention, no-one was ever neglected, when the women went shopping they couldn't walk any distance before they met someone they knew. It was in this way that neighbours looked after each other. This was a neighbourhood to remember, where you could leave your front door open and trust everyone. People were so helpful, if a mother of a family was admitted into Hospital, all her children would be looked after by neighbours. The cooking, cleaning, washing, would all be done by the kindly neighbours, even the steps and pavement outside the house would be scrubbed by neighbours. There was very little trouble over religion, everyone was tolerant, and the children of one religion would turn out to see their playmates of another religion walk in procession. In most streets in Great Homer Street and Scotland Road the people of different religions enjoyed a harmonious relationship with each other.

SHOPS

Before the age of the modern Supermarket the traditional quaint little corner shop was part of the scene in the Great Homer Street area. Almost every street had their own little shop which was absolutely crammed with all sorts of goods from bootlaces to margarine and gas mantles to sterilised milk. People would go to these shops late at night or early in the morning for babies' dummies, sticking plasters, boiled ham, almost anything they needed quickly and unexpectedly. The children went there for their sweets and comics. The shops were open till very late at night, every night, seven days a week. The shopkeepers worked very hard, many of them had started in business by selling firewood when they were children. There was one owner of a tumble down little corner shop whose first job had been selling kewins to the carters going to work at six o'clock in the morning. She sold the kewins for a penny per cup, and had to be up at four o'clock in the morning in all weathers. The proprietors were very proud of their little shops having started with very little. A particular woman had started her business in a little cellar in Hopwood Street. The cellar was in a state of disrepair, but it was renovated and opened as a general shop. The shopkeepers were at the hub of activities in the side streets, they were very much aware of the problems of their customers. These little shops never closed. They would remain open late at night and would be open at six o'clock the following morning. For the deprived people of Scotland Road the corner shop service was particularly useful because the proprietors would allow the residents to purchase a 'halfpenny worth' of a multitude of goods including corned beef, vinegar, flour, syrup and other items which were essential to a family. There was a steady flow of customers throughout the day, and even late at night, the shops were never empty and were referred to as 'gold mines'. Another advantage with the corner shop was that the people were able to obtain goods on 'trust' during the week and did not have to pay for them until the end of the week.

Great Homer Street had the reputation of being the cheapest place in the world for shopping. It was claimed that if you couldn't get a bargain in Great Homer Street then you just couldn't get a bargain. All day and well into the night the street was thronged and busy but on Saturdays it really came to life. There were barrel organs on the street corners, musicians trudged the gutters playing fiddles, banjos, whistles and many other instruments. Late on Saturday nights, the shops, brightly lit, were a flurry of activity as the shopkeepers began to shut up their shops for the day. Mothers out looking for bargains thronged the stalls and shops until midnight hoping to purchase what remained on the stalls at a reduced price. At that time on Saturday nights all the unsold meat would be auctioned. If you were prepared to wait you could possibly obtain your Sunday joint for half the price. In this way the weekly shopping bill would be

Great Homer Street about 1900, the Cow Butter Stores at the corner of Wilbraham Street. This was one of the many shops in the district which remained open very late on Saturday nights.

considerably reduced, and in those days of widespread poverty, every penny counted. Here are some examples of the wide selection of cheap goods available on Saturday nights in Great Homer Street in 1910:—

Beer	1½d per pint
Matches	1½d per dozen boxes
Tobacco	6d per 2ozs
Coal	8d per cwt
Potatoes	3d per 14lbs
Loin Chops	6d each
Kippers	4d dozen
Irish Eggs	1d per 30

Some mothers would end their late night Saturday shopping with a glass of beer in one of the many local public houses which lined each side of Great Homer Street at that time. In their dark knitted shawls and flowered pinnarettes they would sit quietly in the 'side passage' of their local pub out of sight of their husbands who were probably drinking in the bar of the same pub. The men would buy salt fish from the shops on the way home from the pub. It was usual for the families to have salt fish for Sunday's breakfast.

Great Homer Street looking towards the North Market.

In 1910 money was very short and some large families had to exist on a few shillings each week. Their food had to be cheap but substantial. It was claimed that the food in the 'old days' was much more nourishing than today's modern foods. People made their own soups and seasoned them with herbs. When 'scouse' was made the smell of it cooking was very appetising. Favourite meals at that time were:— pig's cheek (half a pig's head) stew, spare ribs, boiled beef and carrots, and pea soup. If the father was working, Sunday dinner for the family would be ribs, cabbage and potatoes. In those days housewives could buy a pig's cheek, 5lb of potatoes, and a cabbage for 10d (4½p). There was no such thing as micro-wave ovens for cooking, people cooked their meals on a gas ring. Some people took their dinner to the local bakehouse to be cooked; the smell from that bakehouse was mouth watering.

About 1914 there were many porkshops in the area. One of the best known was Stanton's. Children would be sent there with a jug for two pence worth of spice balls with gravy. There was a similar shop in Currie Street where you could purchase pig's cheek and cabbage until midnight on a Saturday night. At the top of Doncaster Street there was a cooked meat shop called Rieglers which was run by a German family. People could obtain a good wholesome meal here for two pence (1p). The business was discontinued at the outbreak of the first world war in 1914. Another shop which was popular with the poorer people on Saturday nights, was Sharp's at the corner of Penrhyn Street and Great Homer Street. After all the meat had been auctioned all the left over bones would be used to make the most delicious soup. People would come with jugs, and no matter what size the container was, it would be filled — free. There were premises in Athol Street which were known locally as 'Maggie Blocks' and to which many public

Gordon Street.

house customers went when the pubs closed. Prices here were most reasonable, in 1910 you could buy a meal which consisted of:— potatoes (½d), cabbage (½d), pig's cheek (1d), rib (1d), thick pea soup (½d), blackcurrant tart (2½d). You can well understand why there was always a queue outside this shop, with prices like these. There were facilities in the back of the shop where, if you wished, you could sit down and enjoy your meal in comfort — all at no extra cost. Further down Scotland Road — at the corner of Wellington Street — late on Saturday nights there stood what was known as the 'scouseboat'. This was a steaming cauldron of stew. A fat lady dispensed plates of the stew to hungry customers for one halfpenny per plate.

Before the first world war, barbers' shops in Great Homer Street employed various 'tricks of the trade' to attract young customers. There was one barber with premises near the Homer Cinema, who would cut boys' hair for one penny, then, as a discount, he would give the boy some marbles. Another well known barber's shop near Collingwood Street, offered barley-sugar sticks to potential customers.

There was another well known barbers' shop in Scotland Road. The proprietor was known as 'Billy the Barber'. His customers were all manner of people including Chinese, Red Indians, and an assortment of foreign seamen. Mr. William Roberts had his barber's shop in Bostock Street and the genuine Red Indians, who performed at the nearby Rotunda Theatre, were regular visitors to his shop. He would charge one penny for a shave, and a haircut was two pence.

Liberace — the world famous American pianist talked about an antique shop in Scotland Road. He bought his antiques from a well known woman in Scotland Road who purchased them from some of the big houses on Merseyside. The shop was managed by Miss F. Maitland and the second-hand shop was situated at the corner of Maddox Street. A former beat policeman, who walked the Scotland Road area for many years, remarked that although the shop did not look much from the outside, with its drab brown paintwork, Miss Maitland kept very good quality antiques. She would never sell inferior stock to her clients. In 1960, when Liberace was appearing at the Liverpool Empire, he took a walk down Scotland Road to Maitland's Antique Shop. He caused such a stir that police had to be called in to control the crowds which gathered in the vicinity of the old second-hand shop.

Daly's Tobacconist has been in Scotland Road since about 1897. The business was established by a James Daly from Dunleer, County Louth in Ireland. Unlike the thousands of other Irishmen who had come to Liverpool looking for work he was already employed as a Shore Superintendant by the Dundalk — Newry Steam Packet Company. At this time the cholera epidemic was rampant in the Scotland Road area, people were dying like flies. James Daly was so appalled at the exhorbitant charges of funerals for the Irish immigrants that he resigned his

Children playing the popular game of 'Jacks and Ollies' on the pavement in Richmond Row 1890.

position and established the business of Daly the Undertakers. He had a slogan at the time — 'Respectable funerals at respectable prices'. It was in later years that he opened the well known tobacconist shop near to Cooksons.

McShane's shop at the corner of Latimer Street and Athol Street was the birthplace of Kitty McShane who later became one of the world famous Tiller Girls. Kitty was the daughter of the proprietor and was only a young girl of eighteen when she appeared in the dancing troupe at the Rotunda Theatre. She later appeared with the world famous George Formby at the Olympia Theatre.

'Harry Nicks' ice cream shop was near to Woodstock Gardens. The proprietor was a character, very popular with the people in the area. He was an old, bald-headed man who was very kind to the children from poor backgrounds. On cold winter nights the policemen on beat patrol in Scotland Road would be able to slip into the shop for a warm, a smoke and a very welcome cup of tea.

Some of the better known shops in the district in 1914 were:— Scott's, Syke's, Lunt's, Blackledge's, Pegram's, Maypole, Higgin's, Fusco's, Noble's, Ginsberg's and the famous Duffy's chandlers at the bottom of Rose Vale.

One of the many 'fish & chips' shops which were to be found in the narrow side streets off Great Homer Street. The one featured here was in Conway Street.

STREET BOOKIES

In the years before betting shops were introduced almost every little street off Great Homer Street and Scotland Road had its own 'street bookie'. This was the man who would take the betting slips whilst standing inconspicuously in a back-entry, out of sight of the local policeman. Each 'bookie' had his own look-out. This was a local man who would take up a position on the street corner and keep a sharp look-out for approach of the police. But in spite of these 'doucies' as they were called, the Detectives in the local police station —'Athol Street and Rose Hill were masters at taking the 'bookies' by surprise. The 'bookie' would be approached by what appeared to be a coalman or an ice-cream salesman but it would in fact be a Detective in disguise. If there was sufficient evidence the 'bookie' would be arrested and charged — taking bets was an offence.

Very few people had the luxury of a writing pad and therefore the bets would be written on any old piece of paper — on the backs of empty cigarette packets or soap powder packets. All the local punters had their own nom-de-plume (identifying initials) on the bottom of the betting slip. For example, there was the ex-Corporal who had served sixteen years in the regular Army his nom-de-plume was 'N.C.O. 16'. Another example was a barmaid in a local pub, her name was Bella and she lived in number twenty seven. On the bottom of her bet she wrote 'BELL 27'. There were many amusing names on the betting slips but no matter how unusual they appeared to sound every one of them immediately identified the punter to the 'bookie'. This was particularly useful when there was 'money to

Richmond Row, 1890.

come back' from a winning bet. The most vivid memory I have of the 'street bookies' was during my last week at school in 1951. I was returning down Kew Street to St. Anthony's school in Newsham Street. A very well known local 'bookie' was taking bets in his usual spot on the tenement landing. He was very engrossed in his work and unsuspectingly accepted a bet from a uniformed 'gas-man' complete with bag. It was not unusual for gas-men or postmen or the like to have a flutter but, on this occasion, the 'gas-man' was a Detective. Having had the 'bookie' accept his bet he 'collared' the unfortunate man and took him to the bridewell.

1927. Great Homer Street.
One of the famous Mary Ellens carries
a basket of mistletoe on her head.

MARY ELLENS

The 'Mary Ellens' — the fruit sellers of Scotland Road — were quite a familiar sight in the area many years ago. Dressed in big pleated skirts very tightly nipped in at the waist and worn with a linen apron, they wore salmon coloured blouses and dark neck shawls. The women, with their familiar calls, sold fruit, flowers and vegetables from their handcarts that stood on every street corner in Great Homer Street. Most of the women worked from handcarts but there were some who sold their wares from huge baskets. The apple-cheeked 'Mary Ellens' worked long hours and were out-of-doors in all weathers. They could be seen early each morning pushing great heavy over-laden handcarts from the market to 'their' street corner. The corners from which they sold their goods, in many cases, were the same corners from which their mothers and grand-mothers had earned their living many years before. The first Monday of the New Year was thought to be lucky, it was called Hansel Monday. The first money given to a 'Mary Ellen' on that day was called 'Hansel Money'.

In 1906 there was one particular fruit seller — a young woman who sold fruit outside the Roscommon Theatre in Roscommon Street. She was a very beautiful woman and was known as the red-haired beauty of Great Homer Street. She was always smiling and singing. At this time the Roscommon was a very popular Theatre and one year the management organised a beauty competition. The young woman was coaxed into entering and won easily.

Many of the 'Mary Ellens' went on working well into their eighties, some of the more experienced women could quite easily balance on their heads a basket containing 56lbs of oranges.

Scotland Road's most famous 'Mary Ellen' must have been little Mary Blunn, who sold fruit in Great Homer Street for many years. She was a very tiny woman who lived in a court in Newsham Street, she wore a knitted shawl and made her living selling fruit outside the cinemas in the district. She would be outside with her basket no matter how bad the weather was, she would sell her fruit to the people going to the Homer Cinema at the bottom of Kew Street, then on the same night, for the second house performance she would be outside the Derby Cinema at the top of Wilbraham Street. She would also find her way down to the Gaiety Cinema at the Byrom Street end of Scotland Road to sell her fruit. Although she was a very tiny lady she managed to hawk her huge basket around the district for many years and provided a very worthwhile service to generations of 'Scottie Roaders'.

Her claim to world fame came during the second world war when her name was mentioned on the German Radio. The traitor — Lord Haw-Haw, whose aim was to undermine the morale of the British people, would mention well known local places and local people in his broadcasts in an effort to add emphasis to his threats. During one of his propaganda broadcasts he boasted that the German Luftwaffe had selected the city as a bombing target and were in fact airborne — destination Liverpool. He flaunted his knowledge of the Scotland Road district by referring to 'Mary Blunn' who sells fruit outside the Derby and the Homer Cinemas. His remarks however, did not scare the little woman, in spite of the blitz and Lord Haw-Haw, she continued to sell her apples and oranges. She continued selling fruit in the area until she died, over ninety years old.

WEDDINGS

Scotland Road marriages were something of an event in the early 1900's. People did not have a lot of money and therefore all the neighbours in the street helped in some way or other. The long wooden tables and wooden forms used at the reception were borrowed from the local Church Hall. Relatives and neighbours lent cutlery and crockery for the occasion. The walls of the courts and the parapets (at the edge of the pavement) were whitewashed. Front doors, windowsills and sashes were given a fresh coat of paint. The tiny living room, where the reception was to be held, would be thoroughly cleaned and polished — there was no thought of hiring halls for the reception. Sometimes a new roll of oilcloth (not lino) would be bought from the stall in Cazneau Street Market, two local youngsters would hawk it along Great Homer Street on the Saturday afternoon before the wedding — their reward would be a threepenny bit each. If there were no new curtains, somebody in the street would lend the bride's mother a pair of curtains. If the family could afford it new wallpaper would be bought and hung with a paste made from 'flour and water', this was long before the introduction of the modern wallpaper adhesives. The ceiling having been whitened, the brass fenders and ashpans polished, it remained only to buy a new gas-mantle; the houses at this time were gas-lit.

On the table at the wedding breakfast would be some very tasty food, there would be ribs, pigs cheek, ham and bunloaf. Not very many couples had the luxury of a wedding cake in those days, the guests in 1910 had to be content with bunloaf. There was always a barrel of ale at 'Scottie Road' weddings, this was usually a wedding gift to the bride and groom from their families.

The brides wore large colourful hats, white shoes and fur stoles. Some young women wore their mother's wedding dress. The old custom of 'something old, something new, something borrowed, something blue' was very prevalent at these weddings. The wedding rings in fashion at the time were simple little bands of gold usually purchased from either Cooksons or Stanleys in Scotland Road.

The groom would probably have ordered his suit from Robert & Bromleys, the well known tailors in Scotland Road at the corner of Alexander Pope Street. Many seamen who were getting married would call here between 'trips' to order their wedding suit. Across the street from the tailor's shop was the public house 'Brittania' this was known as 'Mary Kates' and was a very popular meeting place for seafarers in the district. Sometimes, when the men returned from sea and were enjoying a drink in the pub, they would be approached and informed that the suit they ordered when they were last in the pub was now ready to collect.

The transport to the church was by means of a horse and carriage, the driver wore a very smart uniform and a tall hat. There were many brides who were so poor that they could not afford to hire a carriage. Many a poor, but very proud father, walked arm-in-arm with his daughter on her wedding day from their humble little home in the side street to their local church for the ceremony.

Some of the more popular wedding presents of the day were; brass ashpans, coloured shades for the gas-mantles, holy statues and holy pictures of the saints. One young woman received a framed picture of the 'Last Supper' for a wedding present, the following Monday morning it was pawned to enable her to provide some breakfast for herself and her husband.

The highlight of the day would be after the wedding ceremony and after the wedding reception. This would be the family get-together in the parlour of the local public house. All the guests would be ushered to the corner pub as soon as the pub opened in the evening. The entertainment would be provided by the members of the family, they would play banjos, piano accordians, harmonicas and there was always someone to improvise on a beer tray for a drum with a couple of coins. All the old favourite songs would be sung throughout the evening and when the pub closed the party would be continued 'back at the house' with singing and dancing in the courts until the early hours of the following day.

One of the romantic horses and carriages, seen in Scotland Road against a background of trams. It was in this type of carriage that many young ladies went on the morning of their wedding.

CONFINEMENTS

The neighbourly spirit was very apparent when a woman was about to give birth to a child. Usually all the neighbours were aware of the situation and as usual everyone was ready to assist. The expectant father would have to leave the house when the baby was due and walk the streets with the older children. He would have to wait either in the street or perhaps in a neighbour's house during the confinement. Relations would take care of the younger children, while all the neighbour women would be making some contribution to help. Some would do the washing, some would come and scrub out the house, others would help by doing the cooking, they would all be doing something to help.

Almost all the normal births at that time were dealt with in the home by the local Midwife, who experienced very difficult circumstances. They had to work in some appalling conditions and of course, at that time, they did not have the benefit of modern medical facilities such as anaesthetics and sedation.

SEAFARERS

Scotland Road would be referred to in mid-Atlantic by the seamen on the passenger liners that sailed from Liverpool years ago. If you were to ask a seaman directions to a particular area of the ship, he would tell you that the part of the ship you were looking for was "Half way down Scotland Road" or something to that effect. Scotland Road would certainly need to be mentioned if you were to get the proper directions. The reason for this reference to a road so many thousands of miles away was, that on many of the large passenger vessels, the longest alleyway that ran the length of the ship was known as 'Scotland Road'. All the adjoining facilities branched off this main alleyway, kitchens, laundry, bakehouse, galleys etc — so to reach any of these areas you just had to go along Scotland Road. It was perhaps this reference that carried the legend of Scotland Road all over the world.

S:S. Bactria. Built 1928. Sold 1954.

Many 'Scottie Roaders' earned a living by going to sea aboard one of the passenger or cargo ships which sailed from the port to America and other parts of the world. The White Star Company employed many local men. The family eagerly awaited the father's arrival home after a long 'trip' at sea. This was because when the seamen were 'paid off' on docking day many of them took the family to one of the boot and shoe shops in Scotland Road, usually 'Dicks' or 'Bakers', and bought them all new footwear. In 1890, when a 'seafarer' arrived home after a three week trip, he was able to pay his wife her housekeeping in a lump sum — for the three weeks he gave her £1.10s (£1.50p).

S.S. Bothnia. Built 1928. Sold 1954.

In the nineteen forties and fifties it was the ambition of many youngsters at school in the district to 'go away to sea' or, as it was then referred to, 'to join the merch'. The lads had the impression that the Merchant Navy was a glamorous, adventurous life, 'going all the way to America and back', rubbing shoulders with famous 'movie stars' that regularly made the journey across the Atlantic. Another persuasive factor with the youngsters was, that when the seafarers came home, they were always so smartly dressed, always wearing the latest styles from the 'States'. They usually wore either a blue or brown gaberdine suit, sharkskin shirt with a cut-away collar, a very loud tie with a windsor knot — the tie would always have been 'bought in New York', and the shoes were always very smart modern shoes — usually the latest rage in the 'States'. The fact was, that all these young men were always very smartly dressed and were a credit to themselves. So it was, that people, particulary the impressionable youngsters at school, saw the seamen only when they were 'off-duty' and dressed up always appearing to have plenty of money to spend. Their life style did, on the face of it, seem attractive and when the schoolboys were in their last year at school and considering a career 'going away to sea' was always a firm favourite.

S.S. Ascania. Built 1925. Scrapped 1957.

However, it should be said, that the illusion of the Merchant Navy being 'an easy life' was soon dispelled when the lads underwent rigorous training at the Seamen's Training Unit at Gravesend College. The myth was even further destroyed when the young men sailed away on their 'first trip'. They soon realised that seamen worked very hard whether they served in the catering section, on deck, or in the engine-room. Discipline aboard ship was very strict and seamen had to obey instructions they were given.

But, in spite of it being a hard life, there was a tremendous feeling of comradeship among the 'seafarers' and many young men from the Scotland Road and Great Homer Street district continued to serve in the Merchant Navy for many years.

S.S. Franconia. Built 1923. Scrapped 1956.

Marine and General Store in Athol Street off Scotland Road 1903. The store was owned by Owen Campbell and, as can be seen from the picture, he had quite a varied selection of goods for sale.

JIGGERS

No story of Scotland Road would be complete without some account of the 'back-jigger', the playground at the back of the houses, in which many happy hours of childhood were spent. The narrow back alleyways, with rough uneven surfaced paving slabs, a wonderland of magic with side-gutters and grids. After a heavy rainfall, the gutters in the back-alleys provided a wonderful watercourse for boat races. Matchsticks and bits of wood became racing boats which eventually plunged 'over the rapids' down the grid into the drain.

One of "Scottie's" famous back-jiggers – where the kids spent many happy hours.

Smelly bins were set in the back walls, the dustmen having to use special iron implements to unhook the bins from the wall. The high walls were broken by rough painted wooden back-yard doors. Gaps in the mortar of the bricks provided 'grips' which enabled boys with scuffed boots and torn trousers to scale the walls and sit on top of them in the sun. The back-alleys spread like intriguing mazes between the rows of houses, sometimes it was possible to walk the length of the back-alley on the back-yard wall. In almost all the whitewashed back-yards the familiar tin bath hung from a nail in the wall. Very often an angry face appeared at the tiny back-kitchen window and an irate voice would roar "Get off that wall", occasionally a face would peer round the toilet door at the bottom of the yard and tell the intruder to "Keep off the toilet shed".

When the coalman delivered his coal he was hunched almost double, as he struggled up the narrow back-entry with his hundredweight bag of coal, having to ease himself through the narrow back-door into the coal-place. The ever popular 'rag-and-bone' man, pushing his handcart with the iron rimmed wheels, exchanging goldfish for woollen rags, would wander up and down the 'back-jiggers' shouting "Any old bits of scrap iron, jam-jars, bottles, rags or bones". He 'sang' this rather than shouted it, he repeated it over and over, and to a stranger to the city his call may well have sounded something like, "JARR-RAG-BO — JARR-RAG-BO — JARR-RAG-BO", but to the local people it was a very familiar sound in the 'back-jiggers' of Great Homer Street.

GAMES & PASTIMES

In spite of all of to-day's modern facilities, the children have lost some of the pleasures of the simpler things which gave children so much enjoyment years ago. Despite the grim conditions which prevailed in the district, the children were happy to make their own fun. To see a group of these children at play belied the fact that they came from poor homes.

Some of the favourite pastimes for the folk of 'Scottie Road' were:—
Hopscotch. This was a popular game, played on the pavement outside the house. The squares were chalked out and numbered one to ten. The players threw their 'markers' — usually a small stone, and attempted to land on square one to start. Then the player would 'hop' to square one without standing on any other square. In his next 'throw' he would aim for square two, then square three, and so on until square ten was reached and the game ended.

Hopscotch was one of the most popular games with youngsters. Despite intolerable living conditions, these children were quite happy to make their own fun and played together for hours.

Jumping Walls. Playing on the walls in the 'back-entry'. This was a popular pastime with both girls and boys. The kids would 'jump' the walls which divided the back-to-back houses. This was rather a dangerous practice and very often someone would fall off the wall and would need to be taken to the Stanley Hospital for treatment.

Lamp Post Swing. The children would throw a stout rope around the ladder support arm of the lamp post. Sometimes an old 'mack' would be placed on the rope to make a comfortable seat. The children would 'swing' around the lamp-post for hours on end in the summer evenings.

Steering Carts. All the lads had 'steering carts', commonly known as 'steeries'. These were go-carts which had been knocked together from an old wooden box from the market and some unwanted pram wheels. A length of cord was carefully located at each end of the front axle. This enabled the 'driver' to steer his means of transport around the cobbled back-streets. Sometimes on a Saturday morning the 'vehicle' would be used by the proud owner to transport the groceries back from the shops.

Skipping-Rope. Skipping-ropes were an all time favourite with the girls. Every little girl had a skipping-rope and they would skip away in the school-yard or outside their own front door with their friends with not a care in the world. As they skipped, they would sing the appropriate skipping song. One of the favourites, handed down from generation to generation of children, was 'One, Two, Three, Four, You missed the rope, if you miss the rope you're out'. Another old favourite where a group of girls were skipping was 'Call in your very best friend'. It was nice to see so many of the teachers in school getting involved with the activities at 'playtime' in the school-yard. Usually the teachers would 'take an end' each and would 'turn up' the rope to enable the girls to participate to a greater extent.

Ollies or Marbles. Scotland Road claimed to be the original course for the famous Liverpool pastime known as 'Three Hole Ollies' or 'Marbles' which was very popular for many years in the city and, of course, it produced its stable of 'Scottie Road' champions. It was a recognised sporting activity in the area during the depression years and was staged on a piece of waste land near Mile End (between Tenterden Street and St. Martin Street). The land was later developed to build a petrol station. The marbles were made of stone and had fancy markings. The players had to complete a course of three holes which had been dug out of the ground with a pen-knife. The games were played for coppers, pints of beer, or cigarettes depending on the weatlth of the participants. When a player holed successfully, he had the option of knocking his opponents marble as far away as possible and then take a 'free-shot' for the next hole. His opponent would have to make an effort to remain in the competition but despite his efforts he could be knocked back into the 'wilderness' again if luck was still with the

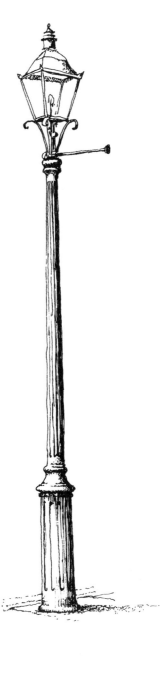

Scotland Road 1908. Showing the old property between Tenterden Street and St. Martin Street. These buildings were subsequently demolished and it was on this "waste-land" that Scotland Road's famous "Ollie Championships" were played.

47

A group of children outside a corner shop in Great Homer Street. One of the little girls clutches her skipping rope. Skipping was a favourite pastime for the girls about 1890.

leading player. This could continue until the player 'in form' comfortably completed the course. The game attracted a large number of spectators which generated a great deal of interest in the game. Many of the little corner-shops stocked the ollies and marbles and some shops exhibited notices which claimed to be 'Suppliers to Scotland Road Three Hole Champions'.

Other favourites were 'Lally-O', 'Kick-the-Can' and 'Rounders'. In the summer evenings in the cobbled streets the older women came out in the street to participate in the game. Teams would be selected and the 'bases' would be identified as 'the lamp post', 'the stable door', 'the telegraph pole' and the 'down spout'. The game would continue until it became too dark to play.

In the early 1900's the lads in the area would 'dress up' to entertain the passengers on the open-topped trams. On sunny Sunday afternoons it was really fun, the lads would 'dress-up' in various outfits and perform their acts on the side-walks. The passengers on the top deck of the trams would throw coins to the 'entertainers'.

Another favourite with the lads in the district at that time was to place metal beer bottle tops on the tram-lines. The trams would come along and squash the bottle tops perfectly flat. The lads would put these 'discs', as they then were, in the chocolate machines in Lime Street Station or in the machines at the Pier Head.

Children playing outside a Pub in a side street off Scotland Road 1890.

Scotland Road – about 1914.

Champion Whates Lodging House

Before 1975, if you had asked any 'seafarer' "Which is the most famous 'doss-house' in the world?", he would probably have answered "Champion Whates in Liverpool". The lodging house was in Scotland Road on the corner of Taylor Street, near the Rotunda Theatre. Generations of people travelling down Scotland Road on the tram-cars and buses have noticed the sign 'Champion Whates — Good Beds' over the front of the building. The lodging-house opened about 1905, and was a large square building which had many tiny windows. It provided shelter to the down and outs for many years. Some of the inhabitants of the lodging-house had been there for many years. Yet no-one could answer the question "Who was Champion Whate?". People wondered whether there had in fact been such a person, was he a genuine champion, if so, champion of what? The oldest people in the neighbourhood could not provide the answer. Some grandmothers, who had played in Taylor Street, as children confirmed that the lodging-house had always been known as 'Champs'. Some pensioners who had delivered newspapers in the street fifty years ago could not recall ever seeing the 'Champion'.

Some people can remember when they were passing the lodging-house very early in the morning, looking down into the basement through the windows, to see a line of sleeping men, all of them draped across a strong two inch rope which had been stretched across the room. This is where the expression came from when people say "I am tired enough to sleep on a clothes line". When it was time to turf the lodgers out in the morning the line would be very abruptly let down. The men sleeping on the rope were the unfortunates who did not have the price of a bed for the night. There was usually a roaring coal fire in the room which provided some comfort to these homeless souls. The rope was referred to as a 'flop', hence the lodging-house was known as a 'flop-house'. If you could afford a bed in the lodging-house in 1915 you were offered a choice of prices — 4d, 6d, 9d, 1/—.

Investigations established that a Walter Whate had been a local wrestler, and he resembled one, for although he stood no taller than 5ft. 7ins, he was extremely stocky and well built. He appeared to have been a very tough customer.

The building, which in the early 1900's was an Army Recruiting Office, was demolished about 1975.

Champion Whates Lodging House.

November 1904. Watched by a group of flat-capped bystanders, a steam traction engine hauls a load of sleepers up towards Boundary Street. Champion Whates doss-house can be seen across the road. There is a barber's shops offering haircuts for two-pence and a shave for a penny.

Paddy's Market

Think of Scotland Road, and you think of Paddy's Market — real name St. Martin's Market, which was established in 1826. It was one of the earliest covered markets in the city and was originally intended to be a retail market with facilities for the sale of provisions and garden produce. It was soon completely occupied by second-hand clothing dealers. The following extract from the 'Daily Post' of 8th November 1883 describes the bustling activity in the market:— *'At the top of Banastre Street a spectacle is to be witnessed which cannot be seen anywhere else in Liverpool. It is a striking example of trade in its most rudimentary form. Here is held what is known as 'Paddy's Market'. Inside this place, about three o'clock in the afternoon, you may see a most extraordinary gathering of tattered humanity. The place is densely crowded by a shouting, gesticulating, swearing, and generally animated mob. Buyers and sellers were nearly all women, and the articles bought and sold appear to be mainly rags'.*

How did St. Martin's Market become known as 'Paddy's Market'? It appears to have been 'Paddy's' almost from the beginning, when the Irishmen arriving in Liverpool went to the market in Scotland Road to buy up all the second-hand clothes and shoes they could afford. When they returned to Ireland they would sell the clothes and shoes to the local people who at that time were living in terrible poverty and were eager to purchase cheap garments and footwear.

In the old days, the market was always packed with people, customers would travel from Bootle and the South-End. The rental for the stalls was only 2d (1p) per yard. You could purchase a warm dinner in the market from the food kitchen known as 'Scouse Alley' which was situated on the floor below the market in St. Martin's Hall. There was a large room with wooden tables and seats which were scrubbed white. The cooking was done on an old fashioned range from which the delicious smell of cooking attracted many customers. In 1907 you could obtain a fine meal there for only 6d (2½p). You could get roast beef, potatoes and vegetables, bacon ribs and cabbage. A plate of good wholesome 'scouse' was 1d (½p) and a balm cake covered with warm syrup — which was known locally as a 'wet-nellie' was one halfpenny.

In May 1941 during the terrible blitz, the market was badly damaged. When the stallholders emerged from the air-raid shelters at dawn and saw the devastation of their market, the place where their mothers and grandmothers had worked for over a hundred years, many of them wept. But these women were tough and had tremendous spirit, they immediately set to work helping to clear away the wreckage and rubble and with their buckets and brushes they soon cleared up the mess. They were determined to make sure that 'Paddy's Market' carried on in spite of Hitler's bombers. Makeshift stalls of timber and corrugated sheets were constructed and soon they were back in business. Even though the roof of the market had been destroyed and the stalls were exposed to the weather, 'Paddy's Market' was open again.

'Paddy's Market' was known to seamen, Indians, Arabs, Chinese and others from ports all over the world. The foreign seamen had no trouble finding the market. As soon as their ships docked they would come ashore to Scotland Road to buy second-hand goods from the market. 'Johnnies', as they were known to the people of the district, always walked in single-file. It was a familiar sight to see a line of 'Johnnies' marching up Scotland Road, one behind the other, all wearing the latest fashion in trilby hats. Trilbies seemed to be a very popular purchase with the sailors and appeared to be something of a status symbol. All the hats would be worn together one on top of the other, until there were as many as eight hats being worn at once. It was said that the 'Johnnies' would re-sell the hats for a vast profit when they returned home. They would also buy old push-bikes and odd items of furniture. There was a particular situation one Saturday afternoon in 1948 which caused some laughter in the district. One of the 'Johnnies' was seen staggering up Scotland Road with a huge old fashioned overmantle on his back. He was almost bent double as he struggled with his burden all the way back to his ship which was berthed in the Brocklebank Dock — quite a considerable distance from 'Paddy's Market', particularly with an overmantle on your back!

The stallholders did a lot of business with the sailors, some of them had 'their own' customers who would return to their stall on each 'trip' to purchase items to take back home. Some of the more experienced stallholders became so familiar with the seamen that eventually they could almost communicate in their language. There would be the traditional bargaining between the customers and the stallholder which would always begin with the stallholder exhibiting an item of clothing and asking the foreign seaman "How much you John, How many

"Mary Ellens" from Scotland Road, set up their "stall on the cobbles" at the back of the market, about 1900.

penny you give?" The seaman would respond with a valuation of the garment which was always much less than that of the stallholders. When the bartering was complete the sailors would grin happily, then clutching their bundles, would walk off looking for their next bargain.

Some of the stallholders had been involved in the market for many years. One stallholder was still active at ninety-five years old and the incredible old lady, white-haired with a headscarf tied under her chin, had been working in the market since she was seven years old. She had begun work in 1887 helping her mother to run her stall. There were many characters among the market people, one very well known personality was Mrs. Cilla White, the mother of Scotland Road's own famous singing star Cilla Black. Mrs. White was tremendously popular in the market and had been involved in the trade for more than thirty-five years. Even when she had moved from Scotland Road to Woolton the ties with the market people were so strong that she would return to her stall in Great Homer Street several days each week.

The old market was demolished as part of the planners' improvement plan but there are still mementoes of old 'Paddy's Market' at the front and rear entrances of Vale View Towers in Woolton. The entrances have been paved with flagstones which it is believed came from the famous market when it was demolished and the paving flags re-used.

Barefooted ragged urchins, selling newspapers on the steps of "Paddy's Market".

Public Houses

The Public Houses in Great Homer Street and Scotland Road had an inexplicable inviting warmth. There must have been an 'Alehouse' on almost every street corner. Many were dingy and badly lit but these were the meeting places — the focal point of the poor people whose squalid lives had very little excitement in 1900.

The Public House provided a form of popular and cheap entertainment. On Saturday nights the 'pubs' held 'free and easies' with a wide range of variety acts to entertain the customers. Many years ago the 'pubs' were open at six o'clock in the morning and remained open until midnight that night. Many a dock worker on his way to work on a cold winter's morning had called into his local for a twopenny glass of rum, only to remain there and lose a days work.

Bevington Bush Hotel.

One of the best known 'pubs' was the 'Morning Star' in Scotland Place. This famous clock-towered old 'pub' was rebuilt in 1862. The premises were referred to in an article in the 'Liverpool Review' of 1888. The article stated that the 'Morning Star' was a subject for fun by the performers on the local Music Halls. A stranger to the city in 1891 described the 'pub' as an imposing looking building situated in a rather rough district. About 1788 the 'pub' had been known as the 'Royal Oak' and was one of the oldest 'pubs' in Liverpool. It is believed that a famous Liverpool Friendly Society had its original founders' meeting in the back parlour of the building. A well known Scotland Road character named 'Dandy' Pat Byrne, was the tenant for more than twenty years.

Another famous old 'pub' in the area was the 'Throstles Nest' at the corner of Chapel Gardens. It was once the yard of St. Anthony's Church. When it was originally built there was a large tree outside the pub, in which there were cages of live throstles. Many years ago there was a manager of the 'pub' named Robert Falvey who was a very good orator and was in demand as a speaker at many public meetings. He also taught languages, and very often, he would orate in Latin to entertain his customers. There is a sad story about a little Italian boy who died whilst he and his parents were staying at the 'pub'. The boy is buried in St. Anthony's.

In the year 1900 there were about seventy Public Houses on the corners of Scotland Road. There was a similar number on Great Homer Street. In addition, there were numerous little 'pubs' in the side streets between the two main roads.

All the Public Houses in the area have been identified with an address. A reference to the street map of the district in 1898 (page 63) will give some indication of the number of 'pubs' in this particular part of Liverpool.

Location No.		Name of Public House	Location No.		Name of Public House
17,	Scotland Place	Cunard House	381,	Scotland Road	Saddle Inn
19,	"	Liver Vaults	393,	"	Corner House
24,	"	Morning Star	1,	Stanley Road	Clifford Arms
32,	"	Old Warehouse	397,	Scotland Road	Rotunda Vaults
13,	Scotland Road	Brittania	417,	"	Brewery Vaults
25,	"	Milton Hotel	12,	"	My Uncle Vaults
49,	"	Grapes	14,	"	Birmingham Arms
51,	"	Coach & Horses	42,	"	Shamrock
75,	"	Swan Inn	56,	"	Bush Vaults
87,	"	Castle	98,	"	Wolseley Arms
109,	"	Grove	132,	"	Clock
145,	"	Black Bull Inn	144,	"	Albion
171,	"	Rose & Crown	152,	"	Market Inn
179,	"	Travellers Rest	166,	"	Grove Hotel
197,	"	Mile End House	180,	"	The Wheatsheaf
229,	"	Plough Vaults	202,	"	Eagle
251,	"	Crown & Anchor	220,	"	The Eagle
259,	"	Bevington Arms	272,	"	Dryden
269,	"	Grapes	330,	"	Eagle Vaults
277,	"	Ship	344,	"	Throstles Nest
291,	"	Grapes	350,	"	Newsham House
301,	"	Ye Old Plough	362,	"	Prince of Wales
309,	"	Globe	370,	"	Half Way House
325,	"	Westmoreland Arms	376,	"	Europa
335,	"	Lathom Hotel	400,	"	Great Northern
347,	"	Parrot	416,	"	Great Eastern

Location No.		Name of Public House	Location No.		Name of Public House
426,	Scotland Road	Gretna Green	59,	Cazneau Street	Royal Standard
472,	"	White Swan	56,	Great Croshall Street	Old Double Doors
484,	"	Hamlet	74,	"	Grapes
2,	Kirkdale Road	Lambert Hotel	67,	"	Australian
22,	"	Stanley Arms	63,	Bevington Hill	Bath Hotel
68,	"	Balmoral	171,	Burlington Street	Golden Fleece
1,	"	Hamlet	143,	"	Cygnet
25,	"	Crown	37,	Hornby Street	Grapes
39,	"	Kirkdale Arms	44,	Hopwood Street	Brittania Vaults
51,	"	The Castle	27,	"	Eagle Vaults
61,	"	Mersey Hotel	65,	"	Ship
2,	Smith Street	Brittania Vaults	32,	Doncastor Street	Doncastor Arms
63,	Kirkdale Road	Goats Head	211,	Athol Street	Trinity
1,	Great Homer Street	New Market Inn	269,	"	White Eagle
5,	"	Old Market Inn	76,	Juvenal Street	Haymarket Hotel
7,	"	Houghton Arms	64,	St. Anne Street	Royal Standard
31,	"	Caernarvon Castle	12,	Gerard Street	Swan
45,	"	Crown	22,	"	Grapes
77,	"	Dryden Arms	86,	"	California Arms
139,	"	Old Grapes Inn	53,	Silvester Street	Royal George
167,	"	Newsham House	27,	Howe Street	Uncle Toms Cabin
189,		North Star	57,	Conway Street	Conway Castle
198,	"	Homer Vaults	79,	Opie Street	Opie Vaults
213,	"	The Clock Vaults	17,	Mellor Street	Mellor Vaults
221,	"	The Derby Arms	20,	Roscommon Street	Farmers Arms
261,	"	Myrtle	123,	"	Royal Arms
2,	"	Queens Arms	18,	Rose Place	Brewers Arms
34,	"	The Box House	36,	"	Eagle Vaults
56,	"	The Elephant	39,	"	Old Dive
76,	"	Clock Vaults	95,	"	Yellow Cottage
112,	"	The Eagle Vaults	49,	Prince Edwin Street	Talbot Arms
124,	"	Oporto Vaults	49,	William Henry Street	Royal Oak Vaults
140,	"	Royal Windsor	32,	"	Clock
152,	"	The Swan	22,	Richmond Row	Mason Arms
174,	"	Foresters Arms	44,	"	Richmond Arms
188,	"	The Buckingham	62,	"	Stafford Arms
198,	"	Jamaica Vaults	142,	"	Grapes
206,	"	Edinburgh Castle	164,	"	Clock
214,	"	Mediterranean Vaults	182,	"	Soho Arms
228,	"	Salutation Hotel	51,	"	Old Gas Tavern
238,	"	The Peacock	65,	"	Albion Vaults
258,	"	Sefton Arms	71,	"	Globe Vaults
270,	"	Candia Vaults	109,	"	St. Annes
302,	"	Caledonian	172,	"	Loggerheads
29,	Christian Street	Shakespeare	183,	"	Shrewsbury Arms
21,	"	Iron Duke	31,	Penrhyn Street	Penryhn Castle
108,	Rose Vale	Stanley Arms	3,	Fox Street	Grapes
8,	"	Portland Arms	19,	"	Royal Standard
14,	Cazneau Street	Swan	28,	Beau Street	The Globe
30,	"	Clock	52,	Upper Beau Street	Old Beehive
74,	"	Duke of Edinburgh			
15,	"	Denbigh Castle			
49,	"	Prince Arthur			

Opposite — Left:
"The Corner House".

Opposite — Right:
"The Europa".

"Westmoreland Arms".

"The Clifford Arms".

"Halfway House".

"The Edinburgh Castle", *Great Homer Street.*

"Swan", *Great Homer Street.*

"Newsham House", *Scotland Road.*

The Gordon Arms.

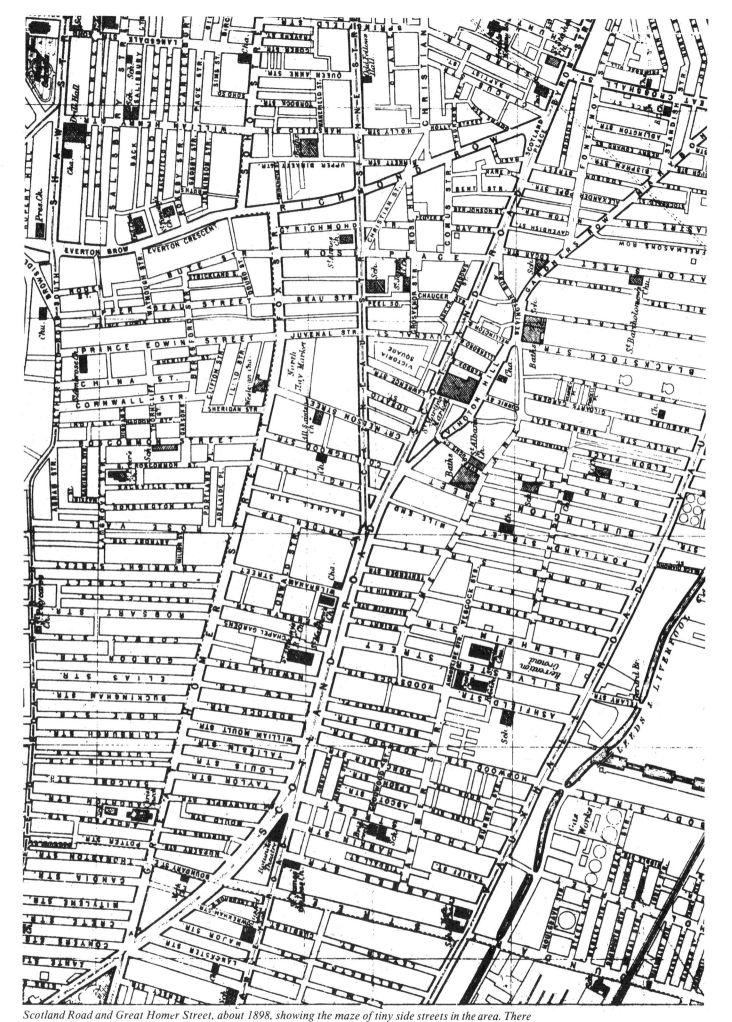

Scotland Road and Great Homer Street, about 1898, showing the maze of tiny side streets in the area. There was a 'pub' on almost every corner.

Theatres and Cinemas

1828, at the corner of Edgar Street, on this site many years later stood the Gaiety Cinema.

In 1924 in Liverpool there were 40 cinemas. In 1950 there were more than 100. These together with the theatres and music halls were a popular feature of the city's social life. The Scotland Road district had its quota of places of entertainment among which were:-

Theatres. Rotunda, Scotland Road: Lyric, Everton Valley: Adelphi, Christian Street: Electric, Scotland Road.

Cinemas. Derby, Scotland Road: Gaiety, Scotland Road: Popular, Netherfield Road: Homer, Great Homer Street: Gem, Vescock Street: Roscommon, Roscommon Street.

Homer Cinema – Great Homer Street about 1940. It was from the doorway on the left that little 'Mary Blunn' sold her fruit to generations of people going to the Homer Cinema.

Adelphi Theatre. Some old 'Scottie Roaders' recalled how, when they were girls in 1912, they used to go to the second house performance on a Friday night. Very often they would see the show without paying. This was because people going to the theatre to see the silent films required someone who could read to sit with them and explain exactly what was happening in the film. The cash box where the tickets were purchased was constructed like a sentry-box. Having bought your ticket you would walk down a long dimly lit passageway to the stalls. These were identified by a large white letter 'S'. A seat in the stalls cost 3d (1½p) and a seat in the gallery (with the toffs) cost 5d (2½p).

Rotunda Theatre. The Rotunda Theatre, or the 'Roundy' as it was better known, was a well known Scotland Road landmark which was world famous until it was destroyed by German bombs in May 1941. The Rotunda was so named because of the 'round' appearance of the building. The history of the Rotunda Theatre goes back to 1854, when a public house on the site organised 'free and easies' each night on a tiny stage in the pub. The shows became so successful that the proprietor — a Mr. Gannell later opened a large upstairs room to present his pub shows. In the early days of the Rotunda prices of admission ranged from a seat in the body of the theatre at 6d (2½p) to the luxury of private boxes at 1/6d (8p). The old concert hall image was eventually discarded as plays became popular. The first pantomime presented at the theatre was 'Jack the Giantkiller' in 1869.

In 1873 a new gallery, balcony and stage were constructed. There were also sixteen private boxes installed. The theatre was so very popular at the time that productions continued uninterrupted throughout the alterations with a tarpaulin sheet being used as a roof covering. There was a disastrous fire in 1877 which destroyed the building. A new theatre was built and opened on 20th September 1878. Bents Brewery took control of the theatre in 1898 and later the interior was reconstructed.

In the old days there were no modern 'show business' facilities in the theatre such as microphones and loud speakers. The artists were wonderful performers, all their words were clearly audible to the audience throughout the entire theatre. In its heyday the Rotunda Theatre vibrated with noise, fun and laughter. The

Rotunda Theatre – Scotland Road 1898. People queued under the canopy and were entertained by "buskers". One of the "street entertainers" was a contortionist.

shops in the vicinity were ablaze with gaily coloured lights and remained open till midnight. Remembering the great days of the theatre one recalls the gaily painted safety curtains and brightly polished brass rail. This brass rail was one of the incredible features of the theatre. It encircled the front of the gallery and anyone who dared lay tarnishing hands on the rail received a mild electric shock from the current which passed through the rail from a battery.

Children considered a visit to the Rotunda as one of the delights of their childhood. They would go to the pantomimes paying 3d (1½p) for the gallery or 6d (3p) for the pit. There was a spiral staircase leading to the 'gods'. This part of the theatre was very popular with children. There was a huge canopy which used to hang along the Stanley Road side of the theatre. This provided shelter for the many buskers who assembled to entertain the crowds waiting to go into the theatre. One of the most popular buskers was a contortionist.

At Christmas time when the pantomimes were on at the theatre the animals from the pantomime would be kept in the stables in Mould Street. There were thoroughbred horses and ponies and, when the circus appeared at the Rotunda, the children would gather in Mould Street to see the elephants being stabled.

Many of the actors appearing in the Rotunda would often call in for a drink at one of the pubs near the theatre. A former licencee of a pub near the Rotunda recalled his experiences with 'show business' people appearing at the theatre. The audiences were mostly Irish/Liverpool people and if you were good they applauded you and took you to their hearts. It was difficult in those early days, you had to prove yourself to your audience. There was one occasion when a comedian was appearing on the show. He wasn't doing too well and the audience was beginning to get annoyed. Someone threw a rotten tomato at him which hit him in the face. Quick as a flash the comic shouted back to his tormentors "Thanks for taking the tomato out of the tin". He described another hilarious situation involving an actor appearing at the Rotunda. A show called the 'Rosary' was being presented at the theatre. The play was very religious and one of the roles was that of a Catholic Priest. The actor playing this role used to visit the public house next door to the theatre for a drink between the evening shows. The customers seeing the 'Priest' complete with collar and dark clothing accepted him as a genuine Priest and greeted him as 'Father'. For almost a week the customers plied the 'Priest' with drinks each night. When it was eventually discovered that he was in fact only an actor calling in for a drink between performances the angry customers almost 'killed' the unfortunate man.

In May 1941 the Rotunda Theatre was bombed by the German Luftwaffe. The roof of the building was one huge assembly constructed of a mass of beams and timber. The fires started by the incendiary bombs took such a hold that it was impossible to extinguish the blaze. The manager of the local pub, the 'Half Way House', was among the many sad 'Scottie Roaders' who stood helpless and watched the old 'Roundy' burning down. The only consolation was that this famous old theatre went out in a blaze of glory and did not suffer the fate of many other theatres which became victims of bingo or the bulldozers.

Even to-day, forty years after it was destroyed, the triangular site the theatre occupied is still referred to as the 'Rotunda' and buses are still using the famous name on their destination indicators.

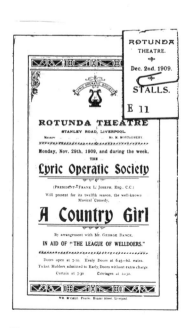

Left:
Programme and ticket stub for the Rotunda Theatre, November 1909. 'Country Girl' was performed by the members of the Lyric Operatic Society and the proceeds were in aid of a local charity.

Right:
The Pavilion Theatre, although not located in the Scotland Road area, was always very popular with residents. Many of them made regular visits to the theatre in Lodge Lane and some schools in the neighbourhood arranged 'trips' to the theatre at Christmas time. This programme is for the pantomime in December 1935.

Horses and Trams

HORSES

In 1900 traffic in the Scotland Road district was very largely horse drawn and it was a common sight to see beautiful great shire horses pulling heavy wagons. At that time horses played a very important role in transportation. Heavy horse drawn wagons were the main means of transporting merchandise to and from the docks and horse drawn trams were widely used. In Liverpool in 1935 there were 4,920 working horses; the Corporation, Breweries, Railways, Docks, Haulage Contractors and many other companies used horses.

What a sight it was to see a team of great shires, the shaft-horse and the chain-horse pulling a heavily laden cart up the hill from the docks. These hard working horses had tremendous power, their magnificent muscles rippling over their huge frame, long shaggy hair covering their fetlocks, iron shod hooves striking the cobblestones as they pulled the heavy wagons on steel-rimmed wheels. The carter, who had such affection for his horses, walked alongside them calling them by their names as he guided and coaxed them along. From time to time he would give each of his beloved horses an affectionate pat as they obediently responded to his gentle commands. In February 1924 two Liverpool Corporation horses, Umber and Vesuvius, geldings of about 16cwt, pulled $18\frac{1}{2}$ tons to set up a world record for weight-pulling. The event took place at the Royal Agricultural Hall. An unforgettable sight in Great Homer Street, in the summer evenings, was the endless lines of empty carts being pulled by the most powerful horses in the world, being led by the weary carter, back to their stables for a well earned rest.

Tramcar 1913. This was the type of vehicle which was so beloved by old "Scottie Roaders".

There were many team-owners in Great Homer Street. There were stables in William Moult Street, Newsham Street, Collingwood Street, Elias Street, Mould Street, Dalrymple Street and Taylor Street. The haulage business provided much needed employment for the men in the district and the early morning clatter of horses hooves on the cobblestones was a familiar sound to the residents in the little side streets. In Dalrymple Street there was a firm called Schofields who supplied mineral waters. They had find big shire horses to haul their wagons. The children in the street where the horses were stabled were very attracted to these lovely animals and knew each of them by name.

Many old 'Scottie Roaders' will recall the excitement of free rides on the horse drawn wagons and carts such as the coalman's or the milkman's. Sometimes there would be the opportunity to sip steaming hot tea from the top of the enamel 'billy-can'. This served the carter as a cup. There was the rag and bone man's horse drawn cart which attracted swarms of children. The familiar sound of the rag man's bugle brought children running from their homes with jam-jars and bundles of old clothes. These would be eagerly exchanged for kites, fishing nets, balloons and goldfish.

Before the second world war May Parades signified a festive time for carters and horses. The horses would be handsomely groomed, tails and manes plaited and brightly ribboned and gaily decorated, harnesses polished, chains and brasses jingling and brilliantly burnished. The carters had tremendous pride in their animals and many of them would sleep in the stables the night before the parade in order to start the final preparations early the following morning. Then the carters, looking very smart in their best suits, would head for the May Day Parade to exhibit their fine horses.

There was a horse dealer in Kew Street who went over to Belfast and purchased two piebald ponies. They were among the first to be brought back to England. The tiny black and white ponies were trained and subsequently bought by Nobletts, the toffee manufacturers. The dainty little animals became a familiar sight in and around Scotland Road. The little bells on the leather harnesses tinkled as the ponies pulled the carts over cobbled streets delivering to the many little sweetshops in the area. The ponies were great favourites with the little children in the district and caused a lot of excitement everywhere they went.

There were a number of stables in Newsham Street and part of one particular yard was used to stable ponies and carriages which were very popular at the time. In 1902 there was an outbreak of fire in the loft of the stable which was full to capacity with hay. The fire was disastrous and many of the carriages were destroyed. The stable was so extensively damaged that the owner transferred his business to stables in Tatlock Street.

There were the funeral horses from Waughs stables near the Rotunda. Groups of men standing outside the pubs would reverently remove their caps and bow their heads as these black-plumed horses passed on their way to Ford Cemetery or Anfield Cemetery.

TRAMS

Children listen fascinated when they are told about the days when trams ran down Scotland Road and were part of the atmosphere. Residents experienced the progression in travel from the days of the old horse drawn trams through the periods of the Oceanics and Green Godesses. The Oceanics, huge vehicles with the doorway located in the middle, and the ever popular Green Godesses, were always a favourite with the youngsters in the district.

Liverpool Tramways were established in 1866 and horse drawn vehicles were followed by electrified trams in 1902 when a training school was established for drivers. The introduction of trams was quite a novelty to the people of Scotland Road. Local schoolchildren would play truant and earn money by entertaining the passengers on the trams. There were many 'toffs' using the trams which ran along Scotland Road in those days and the lads playing truant would dress up as clowns, paint their faces and turn cartwheels on the pavements to amuse the 'gentlemen' on the open top deck of the trams. The passengers were delighted and would throw coppers to the boys. One of the local priests, Father Newsham from St. Anthony's, was forever apprehending the 'entertainers' and escorting them back to school.

Before the introduction of the Green Godesses the driving controls on the trams consisted of a short handle which controlled the supply of power from the electric motors. There were times when this would be thrown into reverse to effect an emergency stop. The handbrake was operated by a cog wheel and ratchet facility. Observers standing at the bottom of Everton Valley near the

Market Official and small horse and cart, North Hay Market, Great Homer Street 1890.

Lyric Theatre would see the driver feverishly winding the handle controlling the brakes, his right foot stamping on the pedal to allow sand to pour in front of the wheels. The warning bell, also operated by a foot-pedal in the floor, clanged away as the tram descended the steep slope towards Kirkdale Road.

At various points in Scotland Road the local 'Mary Ellens' boarded the trams loaded with baskets of flowers, oranges and apples, sticks of rock and toffee apples. These items would be sold at the Pier Head and on the ferry boats. On the return journeys, in the long summer evenings, the 'Mary Ellens' would lead a continual sing-song on the trams all the way from the Pier Head as the trams rattled their way up Scotland Road. By 1930 the trams passing up Scotland Road, their paintwork gleaming, had become increasingly popular as a means of transport. Some years before, about 1928, it was estimated that during a peak hour there were 396 tram-cars per hour passing the Town Hall.

It was a common occurence for passengers to see flames coming up through the floorboards of the tram. This was due to the electric leads becoming ignited. The driver would usually try to deal with this emergency himself by simply lifting up the floorboards and pouring the cold tea from his 'billy-can' to put out the fire. There were times when the drivers were not always succesful and a number of tram-cars were lost in fires.

In many families it was the tradition to work on the trams. Many sons followed their fathers on the trams and in 1914 there was a young driver from Great Homer Street who fell in love with his young conductress from Burlington Street. They were married in All Souls Church and lived in Virgil Street. In 1939 the wages for a driver were about £3 per week; his uniform, of which the drivers were very proud, was provided free.

Since the passing of the old trams, gone forever are the once familiar sound of the whine of steel wheels against steel rails as the trams negotiated the sharp bends at Byrom Street, Great Crosshall Street and Everton Valley. Gone also is the sound of the slap of the leather strap as the conductor rang the bell. On cold winter nights the snow and ice would freeze the points in Scotland Road, the trams were unable to move until the points had been cleared.

In the old days great queues of tram-cars bumped and banged their way each day along Scotland Road to and from the depots at Spellow Lane and Litherland, the conductor calling out the names of the tram stops as the tram continued along the most famous road in the world:— 'Boundary Street . . . Rotunda . . . Hopwood Street . . . Silvester Street . . . Mile End . . . Juvenal . . . Rose Place . . . Byrom Street' and so on.

In the mid-fifties the tram-cars were replaced by buses. The last tram ran in September 1957 but in many a memory there will always be trams clanging along Scotland Road and the conductor will continue to shout out all the old familiar names.

Hard working Shire horse very popular with Scotland Road residents.

Christmas in Scotland Road

Christmas in 1876 was not a very happy time for the deprived people of Scotland Road. Poverty and suffering was very apparent in the slums and alleys of the district. People were being admitted to the city workhouse at an alarming rate. There were 2,262 people including over 1,000 sick and infirm in the workhouse on Christmas Eve 1876. During the week in the workhouse there had been 32 deaths recorded within a period of a few days.

At the turn of the century horse drawn traffic clattered by on the cobblestones of Great Homer Street. The narrow side streets, foggy and wet, gas lamps flickering in the shadows as Christmas shoppers hurried to the shops and stores. The shopkeepers were very busy, their wooden fronted shops illuminated by gas-jets. The people who were lucky enough to have money crowded into the shops, those unfortunate to have none simply stood and thought about what might have been. Barefooted hungry children, shivering in the cold, gazed longingly at the gas-lit displays of food, warm clothing and footwear.

Although Christmas was always an exciting time for children, it was a very busy time for mothers. There was so much work to be done. The curtains would be taken down, washed and ironed and quickly re-hung. Brass fenders, and the ever popular 'home sweet home' ashpans, would be brightly polished. The old fashioned grate would be freshly black-leaded with 'Zebo' grate polish from the familiar black and yellow tin. The traditional piece of mistletoe would be hung over the mantle shelf. The children sitting in front of a blazing coal-fire, later in the evening on Christmas Eve,would hang up their father's sock. The following morning it would be bulging with tangerines, apples, nuts and new-pennies. Some children whose parents could afford it, were taken to the Christmas Pantomime at the Rotunda Theatre. One of the most popular shows was in 1908 when 'Little Red Riding Hood' was presented.

The preparations for Christmas began days before the event, puddings would be made and boiled in a pillow case. A jelly mixed in a large bowl would be left to 'set' on the window sill overnight. Nobody had the luxury of a fridge in their homes in those days. The jelly would be served with custard on Christmas Day.

On Christmas Eve there would be long queues of people either side of Skillicorns Bakery in Limekiln Lane. People who were able to afford a turkey or a chicken for their Christmas dinner would wait in the queue to put their uncooked meal in the large bakehouse ovens. They would return later to collect them. Some poor families were so proud that they would sharpen their carving knives on the door steps to give their neighbours the impression that they were preparing to carve the turkey for Christmas dinner, instead all many of them had was egg and chips. It was the tradition that every member of the family sat down to dinner on Christmas Day no matter how little there was to eat.

Many years ago Coopers vans could be seen in the side streets of Great Homer Street delivering Goodfellow parcels to the many families who lived in poor circumstances. These poor people were very grateful for these food parcels, particularly in the families where there were a large number of children, because very often the food contained in the parcel was the only food in the house. Without the Goodfellow assistance their Christmas Day would have been very miserable indeed.

Older people look back on happy childhood memories of white Christmases spent in Scotland Road, when the side streets took on a white wonderland image. The tin bath on the back-yard wall covered in snow, the clothes line bedecked with white until the snow was dislodged. There would be snowball battles on the way to school. Happy laughing children arrived in their classrooms, soaking wet, rosy-cheeked and with fingers tingling.

At Christmas time the teachers in the local schools arranged parties for the children. The boys and girls were delighted with these events, the highlight of which was a visit to the classroom from Santa Claus who presented each child in the infants with a gift. During the war years, in spite of limited resources, the teachers did a magnificent job in decorating the classrooms. They were able to make wonderful, colourful decorations from scraps of coloured paper, cardboard and other odds and ends. There would be dabs of cotton wool on the classroom window which gave a realistic effect of snow. The holly and the mistletoe, a lovely, cosy coal fire and the singing of the favourite Christmas carols — 'Silent Night', 'Away in a Manger' and of course everybodys' favourite, 'Come all Ye Faithful', completed the atmosphere. The teachers put tremendous effort into creating a warm happy feeling in the classroom, something the children appreciated, and which many of them would remember for the rest of their lives.

Christmas 1916, tickets for 'free coal' were issued to the poor people in the neighbourhood. Many of them were so desperate for the coal that mothers and young children 'struggled' from where the coal was issued in Burlington Street back to the cellars in Great Homer Street without any means of conveyance.

The residents of Scotland Road did not have a lot of money to spend at the best of times, the additional expense that Christmas brought, made the burden almost impossible. Many people visited St. John's market on Christmas Eve looking for bargains. The aisleways were congested as the people pushed their way from stall to stall. The stalls were full of turkeys, geese and pheasants. There were plenty of oranges and apples and heaps of every other kind of fruit. The crowds of people, some of them very well dressed, were all seeking value for money goods. There were groups of poor children who looked on in awe at the amount of food which some rich gentlemen were purchasing. All the stalls on the avenues were laden with Christmas fare. Here is a selection of some of the prices of the goods on Christmas Eve 1909:—

Turkeys	6/- (30p) each
Pair of chickens	3/6d (18p) per pr.
Beef	1/- (5p) per lb.
Mutton	11d (4½p) per lb.
Pork	8d (4p) per lb.
Rabbits	2/6d (13p) per pr.
Butter	1/- (5p) per lb.
Eggs	124 for 13/- (65p)
Potatoes	11d (4½p) per peck
Grapes	7d (3½p) per lb.

It would not be unusual to find that many of the poorer people had enjoyed rabbit for their Christmas dinner.

Spirits were plentiful in the market, these were priced as follows:—

Gin	2/9d (14½p) per bottle
Rum	2/9d (14½p) per bottle
Whisky	3/4d (17p) per bottle
Port	15/- (75p) per dozen bottles
Cognac Brandy	26/- (130p) per gallon

In later Christmas mornings the children would be awake and out of bed before six o'clock to see what toys and games Father Christmas had brought them. They would be so excited and couldn't wait to get out into the cobbled street to show off their presents. They didn't have time to get washed and dressed. They would slip an old coat or 'mack' over their pyjamas and away they would rush into the street on their fabulous new bike or motor car. Scooters were very popular with boys and girls and on Christmas morning in almost every street you would see a delighted child haring around on a red scooter with bright yellow wheels. Little boys would be running around in their cowboy suits, little girls in nurses outfits pushing dolls in prams. Also popular with boys were boxes of brightly painted lead soldiers, forts, drums and train sets. Sometimes the heads of the soldiers would be accidently broken off but in typical 'Scottie Road' fashion the soldier would be 'out of action' only for as long as it took to insert a matchstick to secure the head back to the body. There were, however, occasions when the head of the soldier would swivel on the matchstick during battle. You would, in these circumstances, have the very comical situation of the soldier firing his rifle in one direction whilst facing the opposite way! The traditional favourites, of course, were roller skates and for the boys, footballs.

On Christmas Eve in the evening, one of the local jewellers, Jim O'Hare, who was in business in Scotland Road, would sell 'forfeited' jewellery on the waste land in Kew Street. Many people purchased gifts in this way. Favourites at this time were crosses and chains, lockets and rings.

In the 1920's there still remained a great deal of poverty in the area and not all of the children had new clothes to wear on Christmas Day. For many, whose parents were unemployed and were struggling to raise families, their old clothes would be carefully mended, washed and ironed. The luckier youngsters, dressed in their new clothes, immediately after breakfast would rush off to their local sweet shops to spend all their new-pennies. They would remain in the shops for hours buying ice-cream, sweets and lemonade. They would spend their money as though there were no tomorrow.

At dinner time on Christmas Day all the men would go to the local pub and would remain there while the dinner was being prepared. When the pubs closed the men would return to the house carrying quart bottles of ale. In the afternoon, after dinner, they would have a good old fashioned 'Scottie Road' party. There would be banjos, pianos, accordians, mouthorgans and there was always an uncle who could play the 'spoons'. All these instruments would accompany the many singers who gave their rendition of the old favourites such as 'Nellie Dean', 'Schooldays', 'Pack Up Your Troubles' and many more 'good old ones'.

Illustrated Festive Fare brochure distributed in the neighbourhood at Christmas 1940. It contained details of the Christmas and New Year functions which had been arranged for the people of the area by the League of Welldoers at their rooms in Limekiln Lane.

On Boxing Day the festivities would be continued in the pubs. If there were 'seafarers' home on leave they would be enjoying themselves with their families in the top of Athol Street or the top of Bostock Street. Children would congregate in the lobby of the pubs and peer around the doors. The scene before them was one of absolute happiness, everyone was singing and dancing. Some men and women could even balance a pint of beer on their heads whilst doing a step-dance.

Although Christmas time in Scotland Road always looked damp, miserable and badly lit, the many little pubs on either side of the road were brightly lit, packed and very noisy. And if the singing in the pubs was any indication — all appeared to be merry and bright.

St. John's Market in Elliot Street as it was about 1888. Late on Christmas Eve the poor people trudged to the market and waited hopeful that the price of food would be reduced to a price that they could afford. Barefooted urchins gazed in wonder at the amount of food that some 'gentlemen' purchased and had carried to waiting carriages.

Churches

ST. ANTHONY'S CHURCH, SCOTLAND ROAD

The home of so many Irish-Liverpudlians began as a French Chapel when a Father Jean Gerardot had to leave his home in France in 1793 because of the religious troubles. He settled in Liverpool as a French teacher and in 1804 moved to Mile End in Scotland Road. He purchased a piece of land between Dryden Street and Grenville Street (later to become Virgil Street) and built a Church — St. Anthony's, a quaint little brick building, surmounted by a cross. This was to become the refuge for so many Irish people arriving in Liverpool. They were looking for shelter and came to Scotland Road and St. Anthony's.

It was for these destitute people, as well as for the French prisoners of war in the Borough Gaol in Great Howard Street, that Father Gerardot built his Church. At that time there were only three Roman Catholic Churches in Liverpool.

It was said that the French Priest had some knowledge of medicine and performed 'astonishing' cures. He died in 1825 and was buried in his own Church in front of the altar. Some years later, the influx of people from Ireland having continued, the original Church became too small for all its parishioners. It was decided to build a larger Church. The present St. Anthony's, between Newsham Street and Chapel Gardens, was erected and opened on 29th September 1833. The body of Father Gerardot, and two other priests, were moved to the vaults of the new Church.

The funds to build St. Anthony's Church and School were raised from within the parish. There were very few wealthy Catholics and therefore the parishioners had to support the raising of funds themselves. It was decided to have a penny weekly subscription from the working class people in the parish. A Committee — 'The Society of St. Anthony' was formed in 1832. The members were:—

President	Father Wilcock
Vice President	Christopher Dugdale
Treasurer	John Kaye
Solicitor	Allan Kaye
Secretary	R. Chapman
Committee Members:-	Anthony Myers
	Henry Croft
	Edward Blanchard
	George Beesley
	Richard Beesley
	W. Every
	G. Fendler
	R. Gillow
	J. Pike

There was some difficulty at the outset in respect of the land on which the buildings were to be erected. The problem resulted in a law suit and the commencement of the project was delayed. In order to obtain permission to erect the Church and School, it was necessary to enlist the services of a Barrister at Law named John Rosson. The land cost £10,000.

When St. Anthony's Church was opened the committee who organised the sale of tickets for the ceremony included John Kaye, Athony Myers and John Charnley. The cost of a ticket to admit one into the Church was:— Gallery — 10/-: Upper Pews — 7/6d: Lower Pews — 5/—.

The Church can accommodate 1,700 people. There were tremendous scenes in Scotland Road on the day of the opening of St. Anthony's, the roofs of the houses in the district were crowded with people. It was the feast of St. Michael, people had come from miles around for the occasion. The long lines of carriages which stood in Scotland Road on that memorable day were magnificent. The committee had done a tremendous job in respect of the sale of tickets, they had managed to raise the sum of £700. This included a number of collections which had taken place on the day. There had been some donations to the building fund. The Earl of Sefton had contributed the sum of £25 and there was also a similar donation from Sir James Walmsley, later Lord Mayor of Liverpool in 1839 and later a Member of Parliament.

In 1844 Father Thomas Wilcock retired from St. Anthony's after 25 years in the Priesthood. He was succeeded by Father Thomas Newsham, a man of tremendous energy. He was not in office long before he obtained a substantial concession from the management of the North Shore Mills who up to that time had always insisted that all youngsters employed by them must have attended a Protestant School. This rule was withdrawn.

In the year 1847, the year of the terrible plague, Father Newsham himself annointed over six thousand people. His right thumb, used in the application of the Holy Oil, became infected by the fever and turned black. One of the victims of the epidemic was a Priest — Father Peter Nightingale, who died on 2nd March 1847, aged 32 years. He is buried in the crypt of the Church.

Father Newsham retired from his work at St. Anthony's to a country mission at Fleetwood. He was succeeded as Parish Priest by Father Pierce Power.

During the May blitz in 1941 the Parish Priest, Father William Clarkson, was badly injured when he was a victim of the air raids which destroyed the school basement in which people were sheltering.

Father William Lupton succeeded Father Clarkson later in 1941. He had started parish life in Sacred Heart, Aintree. He remained at St. Anthony's until 1948, going to St. Bernadettes, Allerton. He died in 1968 aged 65 and is buried at St. Peter's and Paul's, Crosby. His housekeeper, a Miss C. Garvey from St. Anthony's, remained with him for 25 years.

ST. MATTHEW'S CHURCH, SCOTLAND ROAD

There was a school beneath the Church, a situation which would not be tolerated to-day. Wilbraham House now occupies the former site of the Church.

ST. MARY OF THE ANGELS (FRIARY), FOX STREET

Five Franciscan Monks served the Catholic community in this part of Great Homer Street where there had been an association with the area for over eighty years. Help and guidance had always been available to the people of the parish from the brown habited monks who were a familiar sight in the streets around the market and in the Soho Street area. Their service to the community was much more than hearing a confession, marrying people or baptising infants.

The Friars assisted in many other ways and were deeply involved with the many domestic problems which existed within the parish.

The story of the Friary began in 1870 when a baby, Elizabeth Rosalie Pollard, was born in British Guiana. The mother of the child had been born in West Derby and had married a Government Official. Elizabeth became an orphan at the age of two when both her parents died and she was adopted by her maternal uncle, a Mr. Irvine. Elizabeth took her uncle's name and came to reside with him and her aunt in Liverpool where her uncle was the Chairman of the White Star Shipping Company,

During her youth Elizabeth had travelled and it was during a visit to Italy she became attracted to the Franciscan Order and eventually decided that she wished to become a nun and establish a Franciscan Order in Liverpool.

When her uncle died Elizabeth entered the order of the Poor Clares. Her uncle had bequeathed her considerable wealth which she used to build the Franciscan Church and Friary in Fox Street.

She admired Italy and Italian items. She purchased the 16th century altar and many Italian statues in Rome and had them transported to the Friary in Liverpool. Her ambition was to bring Italy and the Franciscans to Fox Street but although she appeared to have succeeded she never actually saw what she had created because, at the time her dreams were realised, she was in a Convent.

But she still managed to issue instructions from within the walls. If some part of the Friary was to be modified, permission had to be obtained from Elizabeth before any work could proceed. Mainly due to the generosity of Elizabeth Rosalie, the Friary has been able to play a very important part in the lives of the residents in Great Homer Street.

The traditional May Procession around the streets of the Friary parish was a neighbourhood highlight for many years. Particularly in the pre-war years when people travelled from miles around to see the procession. But in May 1968, for the first time, the traditional procession was held inside the Church. This was because many streets in the parish had been demolished for the new tunnel approach and the residents had been moved to houses and flats on the outskirts.

ST. JOSEPH'S CHURCH, GROSVENOR STREET

A terrible disaster took place in St. Joseph's Church on Sunday evening, 23rd January, 1870. A mission service was being conducted and the Church was so crowded that another service had to be held in a spacious room in the basement building. The access to this room was by a flight of stairs.

At about 7.30 p.m. a drunken man disturbed the meeting, the man insulted the Priest and a scene of confusion ensued. It was claimed about this time a man outside shouted 'Fire' and held a lantern up to the windows. In an instant, because of the alarm of fire, the crowd were seized by panic and a fearful stampede took place. Fifteen people were trampled to death or suffocated.

A happier event for the parishioners of St. Joseph's was in 1936 on the occasion of the Silver Jubilee of Father Richard Green. An outdoor procession was held through the streets of the parish when all the children from St. Joseph's school participated. Father Green had been at St. Joseph's for 25 years and was very popular with the parishioners.

On the day of the procession, the afternoon was warm and sunny, the streets in the parish were gaily decorated with buntings strung across the streets. At 2 p.m. all the children were assembled in the road outside St. Joseph's Church, the Irish Foresters and the St. Vincent De Paul band were accompanying the procession. The route was along Rose Place, into Scotland Road, right down Byrom Street, here the procession turned right into Great Crosshall Street, then into Marybone, right into Edgar Street, across Scotland Road into Rose Place and back to Grosvenor Street.

ALL SOULS CHURCH, COLLINGWOOD STREET

The Church was opened in 1872 as a Mortuary Chapel. The building was paid for by non-Catholic contributions. A Mr. Robert Hutchison, made available the bulk of the money — £2,825, the Earl of Derby, Mr. William Rathbone, Lamport & Holts and D.C. Maciver all made contributions of £100 each.

The Church served the people of Scotland Road for almost 100 years, and was closed in January, 1968 to make way for the new Mersey Tunnel. The Church bell from All Souls was installed in a new parish on the Cantrill Farm housing estate.

OUR LADY OF RECONCILIATION CHURCH, ELDON STREET

On the occasion of the centenary celebrations of the Church the parish was beautifully decorated, baskets of flowers hanging everywhere, gaily painted trellis work around the doors of the houses, everywhere was brightly decorated and illuminated with coloured lamps.

There were pictures of the Pope in every window, on every door and suspended from the decorations hung across the street. To stand back and survey the scene from ground level the streets looked like a huge white and yellow tunnel. Hours of hard work had gone into making this fairyland of yellow and white roses. The flagstones on the pavements were whitewashed and the kerbstones painted yellow. The railings around the front steps of the houses were draped in yellow and white crepe paper. There was great rejoicing in the parish and many street parties. There was an outdoor procession led by the 8th Irish band.

Church of Our Lady (Eldon Street) built 1860. During the centenary celebrations the densely populated little streets in the parish were decorated with a mass of yellow and white flowers.

ST. GERALD'S CHURCH, CRANMERE STREET

In 1915 there was some congestion in the parishes. St. Anthony's population 8,000: St. Alphonsus population 6,509: St. Sylvester's population 7,900. It was decided to form a new parish. St. Gerard's was the 40th new Church to be established in Liverpool since 1707.

On Saturday 3rd May 1941, during the May blitz, a statue of Our lady was erected on a stand in front of the high altar. There was to be a crowning ceremony on the following day. During an air raid that night a tremendous blast from a bomb explosion removed part of the roof of the Church and blew in the windows. In spite of this the statue of Our Lady on the stand remained absolutely undamaged among the devastation in the Church.

Holy Cross Church, Great Crosshall Street 1860.
Drawn by G. Burns from an original painting in the possession of Mrs. D. Knibb.

HOLY CROSS CHURCH, GREAT CROSSHALL STREET

In February 1852 Rev. Dr. Cahill, a well known preacher, was to deliver a sermon in Holy Cross Church. On the Monday evening the Church was packed to capacity and the gallery partially collapsed from the sheer weight of numbers of people who had gathered to hear this brilliant speaker. When the alarm was raised people tried to dash back down the stairs towards the exits. A panic ensued and the police were called. The police arrived on the scene but instead of assisting to restore order they behaved so roughly that a riot occured. There was a public outcry and an investigation took place. Later the Chief Constable of the city was dismissed his office for his part in the affair.

ST. BRIDGET'S CHURCH, BEVINGTON BUSH

A vacant building was purchased in Bevington Bush for £1,560, later this building was to become St. Bridget's, and was opened on 27th March, 1870 by Canon Fisher. Father O'Donovan, then a curate at St. Joseph's, Grosvenor Street, was appointed Parish Priest. His first responsibility was to build a school in Limekiln Lane.

St. Bridget's Church, built 1870. Well known and loved, suffered grevious damage during the blitz when twenty people lost their lives and fifteen were injured. The Church, although not a total wreck, was unfit for use and Mass was said in the upper part of what was formerly the Lourdes Hospital. Father McCabe was in charge of the parish during this period then was succeeded by Father R.L. Tobin who had served in St. Joseph's, Grosvenor Street for ten years then as an Army Chaplin for six years. Father Tobin had the formidable task of rebuilding St. Bridgets in the short space of three years and called on the support of everyone in the parish. The enthusiasm of the parishioners was tremendous and the beautifully rebuilt Church of St. Bridgets was opened on 18th June 1950.

St. Anthony's School,
Newsham Street

St. Anthony's, a bleak two storey Victorian building in Newsham Street surrounded by tenements, stables and warehouses, was probably the best known school in Scotland Road. This famous school, whose former pupils included Priests, Teachers, Pop Stars, First Division Footballers, Professional Boxers, Politicians and Councillors, was demolished in November 1970 after serving the community for 126 years. The school meant so much to the people in the district and many of them were very sad when it closed.

The story of St. Anthony's began in 1840. At this time there were few opportunities for the children of poor parents in fact about half of the children between 5 and 15 years of age did not have any education at all. The schools for the poor were pathetic and were no more than tiny rooms. In many instances dogs and hens occupied the same room and the noise was very distracting.

The Society of St. Anthony, having organised the building of St. Anthony's Church in 1833, now made plans for the erection of a much needed school in the parish. A plot of land in Newsham Street was purchased and building was commenced. The necessity for a school in the district can be gauged from the fact that in 1843 in the parish there were 600 children totally unprovided for with any kind of education or accommodation. Father Thomas Newsham was the founder of the school which was built from the one penny per week contributions of the parishioners. The school was opened in 1844.

One of the early problems in the school was the provision of teachers. A group of Irish Christian Brothers were the first teachers in the school. They worked very hard without payment or reward, apart from the voluntary offerings from the parents. These dedicated men did some very fine work for the poor children of the district and continued to teach in the area for the next thirty years. Their departure, in 1875, caused widespread disatisfaction.

When the school opened there were rules regarding behaviour which had to be observed by the pupils. These were:— 'Children must not write upon the walls: Children must not climb on school furniture: Children must not deface the woodwork of doors: The children attending the school are expected to treat the teachers, and each other, with respect: Children are not to use bad language: Children are to avoid vulgarity and violence: Children are to be clean and tidy in dress: Children are to be kind and generous'.

Father Newsham, in establishing the early pattern for the policy and administration of the school, considered the important factors to be:— The standard of education available to the pupil; The relationship between the teacher and the pupil; General discipline in the school.

The school soon established strong local ties with the residents, playing a very vital role in the community life of the parish. The teachers and nuns provided important social support for many of the children who experienced instability and poor conditions at home.

Year after year the school was singled out for special praise by the School Inspectors. In one such report, the School Inspectors Report for 1849, it said of St. Anthony's:— 'The school has to be congratulated on its good fortune in possessing the services of one of the most accomplished and skilful teachers in the country — the Rev. Thomas Newsham who founded St. Anthony's. A visit to the school, four months after it was opened, presented the aspect of a long established and highly organised school. The children were thoroughly disciplined and under the control of the teachers and the nuns — the Sisters of Notre Dame.'

In 1861 a survey indicated that of all the children attending schools in the Scotland Road district, 80% of them left school before they were 12 years old.

In 1866 there were many deaths due to an outbreak of cholera. The children were advised by the school Headmaster not to eat unripe or unwholesome fruit.

Many children in their early teens would play truant from school in order to earn a living from street trading. At that time street trading was a means of survival for many children in the Great Homer Street area. Truancy was therefore a general problem experienced by all the schools in the district. Poor attendances of children between 5 and 13 years of age reflected the extent of the problem. In 1868 a committee was formed by the local authority to examine the problem of uneducated urchins roaming the streets. Arising from the investigation the following recommendations were made:— That it should be illegal to employ a child of 13 years of age who was unable to read and write;

St. Anthony's School & Chapel 1848.

Parents should not encourage their children to beg in the streets; Police should be vigilant regarding the hundreds of children who were involved in street trading and who prowled about the markets and docks; It was agreed by the committee that drunkeness of parents was a major cause of children's irregular attendance at school. The local Corporation susbsequently introduced special regulations which ensured that school children did not participate in street trading unless they obtained authorisation to do so. In addition to which school attendances became compulsory about this time and to some degree the problem was alleviated although the authorities clearly recognised that the indifference to education was due to poverty, with hundreds of families depending on the earnings of the children.

The improvement in school attendances was followed by a review of the level of discipline in the schools. In St. Anthony's there had never been a lack of discipline. Pupils who misbehaved were councilled and if the offence was repeated, appropriate remedial action was taken. Boys were never allowed to walk about in a lazy, slovenly manner, classes being marched in smart military order to and from the school yard.

In 1883 Mr. Patrick Owens, who had begun his teaching career in St. Albans, joined the staff of St. Anthony's. He was to remain a teacher in the school for the next 31 years.

There was a great deal of poverty in the district in 1885 and many of the children in the district were very thankful for the 'Penny Dinners' which were served by the Friends of the Poor in their rooms in Limekiln Lane. There were also the occasions when children came to school having gone without breakfast. The children clearly did not know where their next meal was coming from and it was left to the teachers in St. Anthony's to give the children penny tickets to enable them to obtain something to eat from the local Cocoa Rooms near Taylor Street.

Some interesting extracts from the School Log Book:—

1864 *Jan 4th*	'The school re-opened today after the Christmas Holidays.'
Jan 6th	'Assessment of accommodation. First Class has 50 children, Second Class has 40 children, Third Class — Two galleries, one for girls and one for boys — total children in class 140.'

According to details in the Log Book the Infant's School was housed in a room that was situated 'underground' and was reached by some stone steps which were 'so worn as to be dangerous'. The tiny room was low, not more than 10 feet in height, and very dark. Gas lights were burned all day long. The room was ill-ventilated and there were no separate conveniences or playground beyond a flagged yard, which was the yard of a Young Mens' Society.

1869 *Jan 14th*	'This large Infants' School is well conducted and is of great use in the deprived neighbourhood around it. The defects of light are very fairly remedied by the care that is taken to keep the windows clean and the classroom walls properly whitewashed.'
1870 *Dec 21st*	'A report that smallpox is increasing in the district.'
1871 *Jan 16th*	'George Munsay and Joseph Massey died of smallpox, and Nora McLoughlan died of fever.'
1872 *May 10th*	'Average attendances in Infants' School is in excess of the maximum allowed by the area of the room i.e. 340. This limit, unless a classroom is provided, should not again be exceeded, otherwise the whole grant will be forfeited.'
1879 *April 1st*	'The practice of spitting on slates in order to clean them should be discouraged.'
1882 *April 10th*	'No further grants will be paid to the Infants' School in the present building.'
1894 *April 12th*	'The Infants have now moved into their new rooms which are commodious and cheerful.'

In 1892 Mr. James Atkins was appointed Headmaster of St. Anthony's and was to remain a part of the school for the next 32 years. He was a very capable and popular Headmaster organising the football teams which enjoyed many triumphs under his guidance. He lived in Royal Street near the top of Everton

St. Anthony's School – Built 1844. The school was a very important part of the community, which it served for more than 125 years.

Valley. When his son James became of school age his father took him to St. Anthony's to be educated. In 1908 young James attended the Priests Training College at Upholland and was ordained in 1914. He was a Priest in All Souls Church, Collingwood Street.

There were hundreds of destitute families in the district in 1895. Many of the children in the schools in the area received clogs and stockings from the Destitute Childrens' Benevolent Society. There were still many school children who, after school, sold the famous large pink 'Liverpool Echo'. This was printed in one large sheet and folded into sixteen smaller squares. The newspaper cost one penny and was very popular.

The Education Programme in Liverpool had made tremendous progress and in 1898 the famous Education Offices in Sir Thomas Street were opened. About this time also, many schools in the district were having telephones installed.

In the Infants' School in 1900 the children used slates and chalk to write. There were large squares on one side of the slate for doing sums and on the other side there were wide, double lines for writing. There was a duster which was supposed to be used for cleaning the slate but it was usually a case of 'spit and polish' with the sleeve of the child's coat.

SCHOOLS IN THE SCOTLAND ROAD AREA IN 1900

Name of School	Built	Total Places	Average Attendance
All Souls	1876	734	700
St. Joseph's	1876	1267	1150
Holy Cross	1850	1020	915
Our Lady's (Eldon Street)	1867	1250	1187
St. Anthony's	1844	1380	1250
St. Bridget's	1877	1000	770
St. Sylvester's	1874	1500	1250
St. Alban's	1860	1400	1250
St. Alphonsus	1889	1300	1100
Christ Church	1850	700	686

In 1900 there were still about 10% of the children arriving in school barefooted even in the depths of winter. They would sit in the class room, their cold feet tucked under them, in an attempt to keep warm. On those bitterly cold mornings the blazing coal fire in the old fashioned grate was very welcome.

At the turn of the century there was evidence that school children in the the area were being exploited. Many of them were having to work long out of school hours for very little reward. In 1901 a School Board Enquiry revealed that the children were working from 5 hours to 44 hours per week. Some examples of the money they received was:— 1 boy worked selling laces for 40 hours and was paid 1/- (5p). Another young lad received 3/- (15p) for working 44 hours in a stable. There was a young girl who was paid 1/- (5p) for working 28 hours in a bakery.

Empire Day, 24th May, was always popular with the children. The pupils would be assembled and addressed by the Headmaster. He would explain the reasons for celebrating Empire Day and the growth and power of the British Empire. He would talk about the Union Jack and about St. George the patron saint of England. The children would sing 'Rule Brittania' and the remainder of the day would be declared a holiday. The attraction of Empire Day for the children, of course, was that a holiday was always granted on these occasions.

During the General Strike disturbances in the city in August 1911 the school attendance was disrupted. There appeared to be a general unsettled feeling throughout the district, this reflected in excessive school absenteeism.

In May 1914 Mr. Patrick Owens, who had completed 31 years as a teacher in St. Anthony's, was appointed Headmaster of the newly built St. Gerard's school in Cramner Street.

St. Anthony's boys class, taken in the school yard outside the Priest's House, about 1916.

At the outbreak of the first world war in 1914 some male teachers from St. Anthony's enlisted for service with the armed forces. All the schools in the area were approached for the assistance of the teachers to undertake work in the munitions factory in Cazneau Street. The work involved the manufacture of shells and for this purpose one half of the Cazneau Street Market was converted into a munitions factory.

Throughout the duration of the 1914-18 war there were continued reports of ex-pupils being killed or wounded. Many former St. Anthony's lads were awarded medals for bravery. Eventually, after four long years of battle, the Armistice was signed on 11th November 1918. The war was at an end. Bells rang out, sirens sounded, schools were closed, there was great rejoicing. The streets were alive with excited, happy people. From that day on teachers who had been away on active service began to return to resume teaching in the school. To celebrate the end of the war, King George V granted a weeks holiday to the schools. Armistice Day was to be remembered each year thereafter. Each year at 11 a.m., on 11th November all over the country all traffic stopped, work ceased in factories and offices and people stood in absolute silence for two minutes. This was in memory of all those brave people who had been killed in the 1914-18 war. The people of the parish erected a memorial stone dedicated to the men from the area who had fallen in the war. The stone, bearing all the names of the dead, was erected in St. Anthony's Church.

On 29th July, 1938, coffins and the remains of people who were buried almost a century before were unearthed in the school playground. Some time prior to the gruesome discovery the school authorities had become anxious about subsidence in the area of some of the out-buildings connected with the school. Before the rebuilding operations were commenced it was decided to investigate to identify the reason. Shafts were sunk in different areas of the playground, and in the process of the excavations, workmen discovered human bones and old coffins. These were subsequently removed and placed in the vaults of the Church. Although quite a number of coffins were removed it was not possible to identify any one of them, there was not a brass plate or any other means of identification attached. The grounds surrounding the school were used as a cemetery for many years prior to the acquisition of Ford Cemetery in the 1850's.

In 1938 the dark clouds of war were beginning to form again. After the 'Munich Crisis' an exercise of 'gas mask fitting' was undertaken by all the senior teachers. The school opened on a Saturday morning in August 1939 to deal with enquiries from parents regarding the evacuation of their children. On 31st October 1939 the first air-raid warning was sounded. About this time school children were issued with gas masks and Headmasters arranged lectures on care to be taken during the 'black-out'. As they had done in the 1914-18 war, the boys and the girls of the school made their contribution to the war effort by collecting salvage, paper, cardboard and metals. Also, as had occured in the previous war, many of the younger male teachers volunteered for military service at the outbreak of the 1939-45 war.

In August 1940, when it was anticipated that the area would be subject to night bombing attacks, the Education Committee issued instructions that school registers must not be closed before 10 a.m. if there had been air-raids the previous night. But in fact during the raids that followed, particularly in December 1940 and during the terrible May 1941 bombings, school attendances were greatly disrupted. The situation after four nights of severe bombing resulted in many children being homeless. There was tremendous strain on both the pupils and the teachers. Some teachers had been involved in A.R.P. duties throughout the night and arrived in school the following morning very exhausted. Many parents, in an attempt to escape the bombing raids, evacuated themselves and their children each evening to the safety of relatives' homes on the outskirts of the city. Others took their children and spent the night in the hall on Lord Derby's estate. When they returned the following morning it was usually too late to go to school. During the war years air-raid practices took place each week in the school. Gas masks were inspected and when the alarm for an air-raid sounded the entire school could be safely evacuated to the shelters in less that two minutes.

A large area of the school building was destroyed by enemy action in December 1940 and consequently there were severe accommodation restrictions experienced by pupils and teachers. With as many as 48 pupils in each class it was an undesirable situation which caused great difficulties for all concerned. But in spite of the inconvenience the atmosphere was pleasant and a lot of useful work

The school-yard in winter.

Name EDWARD COOKE

Address 45 WILLIAM MOULT ST
LIVERPOOL 5

Date of Birth 23 · 4 · '36

School Stamp: LIVERPOOL ST. ANTHONY'S R. C. SCHOOL NEWSHAM ST. LIVERPOOL. 5 BOYS EDUCATION COMMITTEE

No. of years in this Dept. 5

Class on leaving 5A.

Special Aptitude

P16637 552

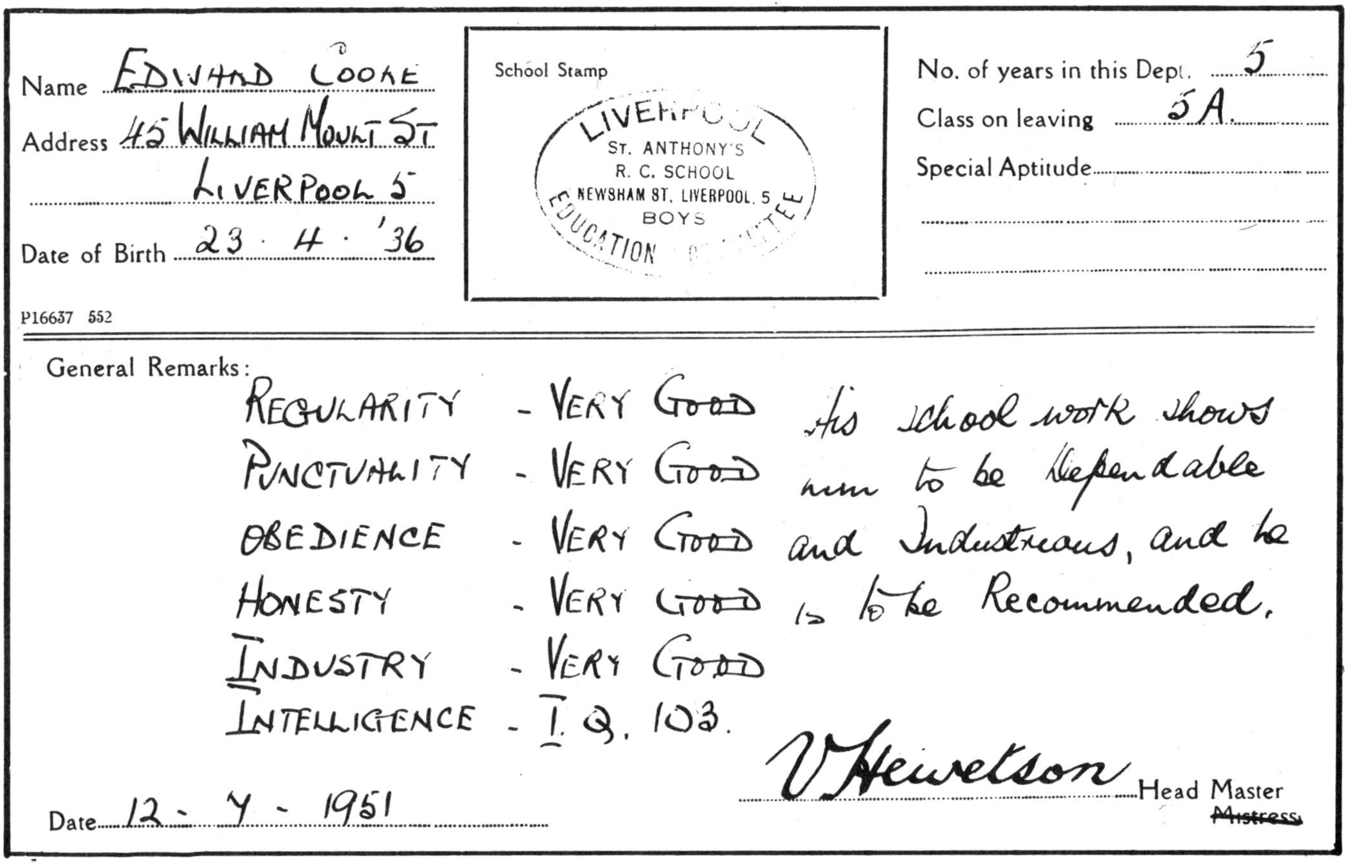

General Remarks:

REGULARITY - VERY GOOD
PUNCTUALITY - VERY GOOD
OBEDIENCE - VERY GOOD
HONESTY - VERY GOOD
INDUSTRY - VERY GOOD
INTELLIGENCE - I. Q. 103.

His school work shows him to be dependable and Industrious, and he is to be Recommended.

Date 12 - 4 - 1951

V Hewetson Head Master ~~Mistress~~

Scholars School Reference.

was being done by the children. The teachers tried to make the children as comfortable as possible under the circumstances. The shortage of accommodation was attributed to the air-raids and had affected many schools in the Scotland Road area. Holy Cross school lost half its accommodation: St. Bridget's school was damaged beyond repair; St. Sylvester's lost half its places: St. Gerard's school was totally destroyed: Part of St. Alphonsus school was destroyed: The top floor of St. Augustines school was damaged and out of use: St. Alban's school was destroyed. The shortage of places in St. Anthony's school prevailed throughout the war years and did not improve until the re-building of the bombed school was completed in 1950.

In 1945 when the war came to an end there was tremendous celebrations in the parish. Many children looked forward to seeing fathers, brothers, uncles and cousins who had been away from home for many years. Above all people looked forward to living a normal life and in the school the teachers tried to settle the pupils down to some hard studying without the constant distraction of air-raids and all the heartache which they generated.

In 1949 Mr. J. Murray, the well respected Headmaster of the school, retired after a lifetime of service to St. Anthony's. Mr. Murray, a 'Military Gentleman', had served in the 1914-18 war and was a strict disciplinarian. He had a reputation for standing no nonsense and had in fact been responsible for 'straightening out' a few 'tearaways' in his time. When he retired from St. Anthony's he said that he had many happy memories of the school and of the generations of pupils he had taught. It was his opinion that the school had been successful and had indeed been helpful to the community it served in Scotland Road. Mr. Murray was to enjoy his well earned retirement until his death in 1979 at the age of 93.

In the late fifties the demolition of the houses in the district reduced the classroom population. Fewer youngsters resulted in an increasing number of empty desks in the school. In its heyday there had been more than 1200 pupils on the register but in 1969 diminishing numbers of children subsequently resulted in a decision being taken by the local authorities to close the school. After 126 years the famous school that had been such a symbol of security in the community was to be demolished along with the many derelict houses in the area. The school had been very much a family school with four and even five generations from the same family having attended the school.

In November 1970, only weeks before the inevitable closure of the school, many former pupils sadly returned to St. Anthony's to have a 'last look' at the place where they had spent such happy school days. They found the school just as they had remembered it, apart from the classrooms which many years earlier had seemed so vast, now appeared very small. The piano was still against the wall which they had filed past as infants to take their places for morning prayers. There was the old fire grate where in winter a cheerful coal fire had burned and, where if it was a bitterly cold morning, the teachers would allow the bottles of milk to be warmed to 'take the chill off'. During that sentimental journey back to the school, ex-pupils recalled the wonder of the school Christmas parties of the past. How the teachers had made such beautiful decorations, the Christmas trees, holly and mistletoe and the wonderful feeling of happiness when the Christmas carols were sung. Some of the older people who returned to the school recalled nostalgic memories of the school caretaker of long ago going around the classrooms lighting the gas lamps from a lighted taper.

Eventually the school locked its gates for the last time, no more children playing in the school yard, no more singing in the classrooms, no more running in the corridors. Soon the school was reduced to a pile of rubble. Scotland Road said goodbye to an old friend when St. Anthony's school was closed, it was the end of a little piece of Liverpool history.

St. Anthony's girls class, taken about 1885.

General Strike
1911

Two men were shot dead by soldiers and hundreds injured in battles with the police during three days of rioting. The trouble began during a strikers' demonstration on St. George's Plateau on Sunday, 13th August 1911. The men who died were shot on the following Tuesday when a mob near the Scotland Road district tried to release prisoners who had been sentenced for offences during the rioting. The prisoners were in police vans on their way to Walton Gaol with an escort of the 18th Hussars.

Police arrest a man during the disturbances in Great Homer Street in 1911.

The events leading up to the demonstrations on 'Bloody Sunday' had begun when shipowners had refused to employ members of the trade union. A strike ensued and subsequently the owners agreed to raise pay and to recognise the union. However, in Liverpool, the seamen refused to return to work until the demands of the transport workers had been met. The railway, carters and other workers joined the strike. The docks were at a stand still and mills and factories were closed.

On Friday, 11th August rioting had occurred in Great Crosshall Street and Soho Street, police were attacked and missiles thrown. There were many arrests made. The tension in Scotland Road was heightened with hundreds of men on strike and food running short. Many men from Scotland Road flocked to the meeting on Sunday, 13th August. The meeting was addressed by Tom Mann, the Chairman of the Liverpool Strike Committee. There were more than 25,000 people at the meeting.

During the meeting rioting broke out in Lime Street near the North Western Hotel. The policemen lashed out with their truncheons and in a few minutes hundreds of strikers were fighting with the police. Police reinforcements were quickly drafted in and a large number of policemen baton-charged the strikers. Later the Warwickshire Regiment arrived to reinforce the police and mounted police charged the crowd. Fighting occurred in Byrom Street and Addison Street. In Gerard Street slates and bricks were torn from the roof tops and hurled at the police. More than two hours elapsed before order was restored to the area. Throughout the evening sporadic rioting continued, some public houses in Burlington Street were damaged. In Sylvester Street a mob looted a bread delivery van. Police sent to the area drew batons and charged the looters many of whom were injured in the clash. That night savage fighting began in Great

Christian Street 1911. Crowds gather outside the Shakespeare Public House, there is extensive damage to the windows.

Homer Street involving hundreds of men and women. The Scots Greys, who were stationed nearby in Great Homer Street fruit market, were summoned to the area to restore order. Shots were fired but there was no one hit though there were many troops injured by flying bottles and bricks. The injured were treated at the Northern Hospital and the Royal Infirmary. Police reinforcements arrived from Lancashire County, Bradford and Nottingham. Cavalry reinforcements were held in reserve in Hatton Garden.

On Monday, 14th August more than 100 people appeared in the city courts. They were all charged with offences arising from the previous days' riots and many of them received heavy prison sentences. The following day there were even more prisoners sentenced to gaol many of them for assaulting the police. That night there were fires lit by the rioters in Dryden Street and Virgil Street.

Many of the residents living in the maze of side streets between Scotland Road and Vauxhall Road were still very angry about the number of people injured on the Sunday. There was a lot of feeling of sympathy for the prisoners and there had been some talk in the district of attempting to release them. A large crowd assembled near Burlington Street armed with clubs and stones.

On Tuesday, 15th August at six o'clock in the evening, ninety prisoners were being transferred from the bridewell in Dale Street to Walton Gaol in five prison vans. The vans entered Vauxhall Road accompanied by an escort of the 18th Hussars Cavalry. Suddenly from the tiny side streets rushed hundreds of yelling men and women. They hurled missiles at the escort and it was later claimed that some people in the crowd had rifles. The mob rushed the convoy and the Hussars drew their swords. The rain of bottles and bricks continued. Some of the rioters ventured forward and seized hold of the bridles of the horses. The officer in charge of the escort gave the order to 'open fire' and John Suttcliffe aged 20, a carter, was shot through the head. He died later in Hospital. Another man attacked a troop sergeant with an iron bar. The soldier drew his revolver and fired. Michael Prendergast aged 30, a dock worker, fell dead — shot through the heart. The disturbances continued along Vauxhall Road but the prison vans and the escort reached Walton Gaol.

The strike came to an end on 24th August 1911, the trade unions winning some concessions. Eventually people began to settle down, tempers were restored and relationships developed again. It was regrettable that many of the young men from Scotland Road and Great Homer Street, who were involved in the riots, died on the battle fields of Flanders during the 1914-18 war.

The 'Loot'
1919

In the old 'Scottie Road' days Liverpool City Police 'D' Division Headquarters was in Rose Hill with a sub-station in Athol Street. These were both very busy police stations. 'D' Division was the toughest of all the police divisions in the city, the men on the beat patrolled in pairs. Drunken brawls were almost a nightly occurrence. Saturday nights were usually the worst and it was a common sight to see offenders being marched to the bridewell in Athol Street between two policemen. The policemen who patrolled the Scotland Road district in the old days, with a baton, a torch and a whistle, had to be tough.

Times were very hard for the people and the policemen on the beat had for the local residents both admiration and sympathy. They were very much aware of the appalling slum conditions in which the desperately poor people lived with no hope of escape from the constant misery and poverty. Many of the policemen were on friendly terms with the local residents. The people trusted their own 'beat bobby' and in fact there was many a baby brought into the world with the assitance of a policeman from Rose Hill or Athol Street. One ex policeman, who had spent 26 years on the beat in Great Homer Street, said "The people from the little side streets in Scotland Road were fine people but they had to live in some terrible conditions."

August 1919. During the Police Strike many shops were 'boarded-up' to prevent looting during the riots. This shop was located at the junction of Bevington Bush and Scotland Road. It was also at this spot that many years previous, the legendary Seth Davy had entertained the children with his famous dancing dolls.

These terrible conditions were blamed for the rioting and looting which began on August Bank Holiday 1919 at the time of the Police Strike. By the end of the Bank Holiday barely a shop window remained unbroken in Scotland Road. Looting had taken place on a massive scale. One local man had been shot dead by one of the hundreds of soldiers who had been drafted into the area to protect property. There were more than 300 people sentenced after the Bank Holiday for offences arising from the looting and rioting.

The background to the dispute was a demand by the police and prison officers for trade union recognition and a wage increase. On Thursday, 31st July 1919 there was a call for a national police strike. In Liverpool, where a policeman's pay was less than a dockers and where discipline was harsh and unjust, there was an immediate response and a thousand men came out on strike. An orgy of looting and rioting followed.

The trouble started on the Friday night (1st August). Eighty policemen had assembled as a mass picket outside the city Police Headquarters. The members of the Liverpool Fire Service were asked to support the strike but this was refused. That Friday night some shop windows in Great Homer Street were shattered but rioting and looting really took a hold on the following day — Saturday (2nd August). All the policemen who were on strike marched up Hopwood Street and along Scotland Road to Rose Hill police station. Later in the afternoon Cranes piano warehouse near Hornby Street was broken into. That evening, when the people began to come out of the public houses, there began an unrestrained orgy of looting in Great Homer Street and Scotland

Road. Drunken mobs ran through the streets, fighting, wrecking shops and business premises. Little groups of people moved from one looted shop to the next helping themselves to the goods. Boot shops appeared to be the targets in the early stages of the looting but later on the looters became more venturesome and pawnbrokers and jewellers shops claimed their attention. The looters were composed of an equal number of men, women and boys but the women were very active and were to be seen coming out of the looted shops with bundles of stolen goods. The smashing of plate glass windows in Great Homer Street could be frequently heard during the night. The lamps were sparsely lit and the looting was screened by the darkness.

A small unit of non-striking policemen were on duty in Great Homer Street and patrolled the area with batons drawn. This did not prevent Sturla's Outfitters being looted and even the carpet from the floor of the store was taken up and stolen. Other shops and stores which were attacked in the district that day were Leylands (outfitters), Dryden Street: Healings (pawnbrokers), Fox Street: Clarksons (pawnbrokers), Scotland Road: Dicks (boot stores), Scotland Road: Leighs (grocers), Scotland Road. In all there were more than 20 shops looted throughout the Saturday night and there were 26 people arrested. By Sunday afternoon (3rd August) looting had become widespread in the district. In Great Homer Street and Scotland Road a great deal of damage had taken place and a considerable quantity of goods had been stolen by the mobs. The Lord Mayor of Liverpool issued an appeal to all law-abiding citizens to assist in preserving law and order.

Women were seen pushing handcarts full of stolen goods. One woman was spotted in Latimer Street by the Parish Priest, he reprimanded the woman and told her to take the property back to the shop. All the Priests in the Churches in Scotland Road spoke out very strongly against the looting which was taking place in the district.

Troops with tanks and guns had been called in to restore order. A battalion of the Royal Welsh Fusiliers were billeted in the Rotunda Theatre. The troops were positioned at strategic points along Scotland Road and Great Homer Street, groups of soldiers patrolled the side streets. The threat to property was ever present, the proprietors of stores in the district, made it very clear to their staff that they expected them to volunteer their services to defend the shops and warehouses against the looters. Many of these workers were sworn in as special constables.

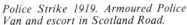

Police Strike 1919. Armoured Police Van and escort in Scotland Road.

During the evening of Sunday (3rd August) rioting broke out in London Road. All available troops, police and specials were rushed to the area. The crowds in Great Homer Street were surprised at the almost total absence of the police and military and took full advantage of the situation. Many shops were looted, pawnbrokers being the main target. One particular pawnbrokers — Brown & Walkers, at the corner of Hopwood Street and Latimer Street, was left completely empty. Gents Outfitters were broken into, men and boys could be seen walking away from the shops wearing new suits.

The police and military were determined to beat the mobs into submission and as soon as there was an outbreak of looting or stone throwing troops were rushed to the area as quickly as possible. It was during one such outbreak that six lorry loads of troops were despatched to Scotland Road and parked in Bostock Street and Kew Street. Upon the order from the Officer in command the troops poured into Scotland Road, and using their rifle butts as clubs, managed to push the mob back down Hopwood Street. For some time the mob was held back and controlled but there were some agitators at the front of the crowd who were urging the mob to rush towards the shops. One of these agitators stepped forward from the crowd and barring his chest, he turned to the soldiers and shouted "Shoot me", "Shoot me". He continued to do this for a few minutes then two policemen rushed out. The man quickly turned and fled before two flaying batons into the safety of the crowd. The agitators continued to urge the crowd to charge forward. A small band of policemen had stood at the alert for some time and as the crowd were being 'whipped up' by their leaders a police whistle sounded and the burly line of policemen, with batons drawn, charged forward into the mob. The crowd saw their colleagues, in the front, fall under the fearful blows from the police truncheons. The baton charge was succesful, the crowd turned and fled. They ran down back-alleys and side streets, they ran anywhere in their desperate attempts to get away from the police who were now being strongly supported by the soldiers. The troops regrouped and advanced on another mob which had formed near the corner of Boundary Street. There was a warning volley fired into the air from which a ricochet hit a rioter. He was rushed to Hospital with a bullet wound in his neck.

Police Strike August 1919. Fires are lit in side-streets off Great Homer Street. There was widespread looting of shops and warehouses in the area.

ROSE HILL POLICE STATION

Rose Hill Police Station: during the "riots" in 1919, the cells in this building were full to capacity. It was also from the bridwell (as well as Athol Street bridewell) that the "police clothing" was issued to the poor children of the district.

There were many clashes with the rioters and the crowd seemed to be intent on marching into the city. The police and troops had been successful in pushing the crowd back some distance to Mile End. There was quite a large angry mob and as the troops had been called away to another outbreak in Great Homer Street, there was only a small body of policemen holding them back. Suddenly a burly police inspector, who had a reputation of standing no nonsense, stepped forward and with his truncheon, marked a line in the road. He warned the mob, "Any man crossing that line does so at his peril. You have been warned". He then stepped back in line with his men. The mob were being encouraged to move forward by one huge loud-mouth in the front, he shouted something then lunged across the line. He was struck down immediately by police truncheons, the crowd halted and quickly dispersed into the side streets. Later that evening (Sunday, 3rd August) there was a mob looting shops in Cazneau Street. The troops and a small band of policemen were despatched to the area and the looting was stopped and many arrests were made. As the prisoners were being escorted away the Officer in charge was informed that some shops near the Rotunda were being looted. A party of troops and police were deployed to the area at once. The Riot Act was read out to the mob and they were advised to return to their homes.

The small band of troops and police were reinforced by a large force of troops who marched in open-order up Scotland Road with fixed bayonets. A halt was called near Athol Street and the troops took up positions along each side of the road as far as Boundary Street. There were fierce battles throughout the Sunday night, near the Rotunda and along Great Homer Street. There appeared to be little hesitation in taking prisoners. Rose Hill and Athol Street police stations were filled well beyond capacity and in the rain of the following Monday morning. Great Homer Street was littered with broken glass. Throughout that day the police and military regained control of the situation, a curfew imposed before dark was rigidly enforced.

The search of premises for stolen property began. The soldiers would come to the houses in the early hours of the morning and hammer loudly on the front door. If they did not obtain an answer quickly the door would immediately be broken down with rifle butts. The soldiers would then make a thorough search of the premises. The result was that many people who did have stolen property in their homes became so afraid of being caught in possession, disposed of the stolen goods as quickly as possible. Many people anonymously deposited piles of stolen items on the bowling green in Silvester Street near St. Martin-in-the-Fields Church.

In the aftermath to the wave of lawlessness that had swept the district during the August Bank Holiday, the Stipendiary was kept busy dealing with cases arising out of the rioting and looting which had taken place.

In evidence it was said that some of the accused had been seen smashing the windows of a boot store, others went inside the shop and were observed passing boxes of boots out to the crowd. A young lad who was walking away with a bundle of six pairs of boots was confronted by a policeman. The excuse the boy gave was that "he picked them up in the street". In court, clocks, silverware, bundles of clothes and electrical goods were produced to substantiate the various charges. A woman who had been arrested together with four men in the doorway of a shop in Scotland Road which was being looted, denied the charge. The detective who arrested her said in court that the woman had claimed "I didn't steal any shoes, I didn't have time to find a pair to fit me".

During one particular case the following words were spoken in the Stipendiary Magistrates Court by a prisoner pleading for leniency before the magistrate.

"Yer honour I have a bayonet wound in me back."

"Do you mean you were wounded in the trenches?"

"O no yer honour, in Scotland Road."

During the riots many local people had been injured. Many were subsequently sent to Walton Gaol to serve sentences. One local man had been shot, Cuthbert Thomas Howlett aged 33yrs, living at 33 Skirving Street and employed as a bottle works labourer, was admitted to Hospital. He later died of gunshot wounds.

Many people claimed that the riots and looting which had taken place was a product of much more than the police strike and had occurred because of the poverty and terrible living conditions which existed at the time. It may have been seen as an opportunity to retaliate for all the empty stomachs, the bare feet and four years of war, with many lads from Great Homer Street and Scotland Road killed in the trenches. Hungry ill-clad people took advantage of the absence of the police to rampage through the street stealing what they wanted.

The Police Strike was eventually beaten and the 930 policemen who went on strike were dismissed from the Liverpool Force. New recruits filled the vacancies and many of the dismissed policemen forfeited their pensions and were 'blacklisted' whenever they applied for employment in Liverpool.

"Dicks" Boot Store in Scotland Road near Wellington Street. This was one of the targets for the "looters" during the Police Strike – August 1919.

Scotland Road at War
Blitz 1940/41

In September 1939 when war was declared the young men of Scotland Road joined up in their thousands. Some sailed under the 'White Ensign' or the 'Red Duster', others shouldered a rifle and trooped off to war. Tragically, many hundreds of these brave young men never returned to their homes in the narrow side streets of Scotland Road.

Those who remained at home worked long hours at their normal jobs during the day and reported for 'Home Guard' duties at nights. During the war years the housewives had to struggle and cope with all the difficulties which arose from food rationing and clothing coupons.

As the war developed, Hitler recognised the immense strategic importance of the Liverpool docks and surrounding industrial facilities. He knew that if he could destroy the port of Liverpool, Britain would soon be crippled. The German High Command ordered sustained air attacks on the target — Liverpool. Scotland Road, being located on the edge of the city centre and alongside the line of docks, was in the front line and therefore very vulnerable to air attacks.

When the war came to Scotland Road families refused to split up, no matter what happened, no matter how severe the air raids were to become, the family would remain together. Many mothers would take their young children and huddle together under the stairs. Air raid shelters were constructed in the streets to provide shelter for the residents. Barrage Balloon Units were set up. These were huge balloons which were moored by steel cables. The intention was that the balloons would hinder the approach of the Nazi bombers. There was a Barrage Balloon Unit located in Silvester Street behind the 'Black Church', 'St. Martin-in-the-Fields', and near to the Gem cinema in Vescock Street.

Throughout the blitz on Liverpool the people of Scotland Road and Great Homer Street took fearful punishment. The air raids of December 1940 brought Scotland Road's most depressing Christmas. Night after night more than 300 enemy planes attacked. The sirens would sound alerting people that German bombers had arrived over the estuary. The residents of Great Homer Street and Scotland Road trooped wearily each night to the air raid shelters. There were many weary, sleepless nights as the exploding bombs shook the structure of the shelters. As daylight approached it brought the welcoming sounds of the 'all clear' and in the chill morning air the people dragged themselves out of the shelters and climbed over rubble hopeful that their homes would still be standing. Thousands of people saw their homes destroyed during the bombing.

During the many air raids on Scotland Road the residents demonstrated their determination not to 'give in'. One night the water supply failed making fire-fighting impossible. The people in the Boundary Street area used tarpaulin sheets to erect emergency water tanks in the street. The children then formed a human chain and passed buckets of water from the Leeds—Liverpool canal (which ran through Boundary Street) to fill the tarpaulin tanks. The fire-fighters were then able to utilise the tanks to control the outbreaks of fires in the area.

During an air attack on Saturday 21st December 1940 two Priests, together with parishioners, were killed when a bomb made a direct hit on the club rooms under St. Anthony's school in Newsham Street.

During the raid many dwelling houses were demolished by high explosive bombs. Residents in Newsham Street tackled the incendiary bombs which had become embedded in the roof tops causing numerous fires. Among those killed in the school were two Catholic Priests, Father O'Keefe and Father Kavanagh, a young soldier James Grant, who was on leave and the school caretaker Alex Thompson and his wife Margaret, their children, Margaret aged 12, Joan aged 7 and Tony aged 4½. The family lived in William Moult Street and had gone into the school basement seeking shelter from the bombing. Father William Clarkson, Parish Priest of St. Anthony's, was one of four people rescued from the building. He was badly injured and spent a considerable time in hospital.

21st December 1940 was the last time that Holy Mass was celebrated in the old Holy Cross Church in Great Crosshall Street. Priests and parishioners fought bravely to save their church but in spite of the fearless courage of the fire-fighters Holy Cross, hit by a shower of incendiary bombs, went up in flames. As burning embers fell from the roof parishioners helped Father Doyle to move sacred vessels and vestments from the blazing church to the safety of nearby houses. Father Doyle and Father Morrison, clad in their pyjamas and top coat, were operating stirrup pumps and doing everything they could to control the fire. But it was to no avail. Soon this fine old church was reduced to a twisted mass of blackened wreckage. The following morning, in the chill dawn, the German bombers gone, groups of Holy Cross parishioners gathered and wept bitterly.

The air raids continued each night, each raid for a longer duration than the previous one. On 12th March 1941 the parish of Holy Cross was again under attack when parachute mines fell on Lace Street and Adlington Street. Numerous homes were destroyed and many people buried beneath the debris. A parachute mine, which landed on the shelter of Holy Cross School in Adlington Street, killed 125 people. Rescue workers tore at the rubble with their bare hands in a desperate attempt to reach survivors. Even while they were doing this enemy planes flew low overhead with machine guns blazing at them. The Priests from Holy Cross worked throughout the night annointing the many dying and comforting the suffering. There was one occasion when rescue workers assisted a Priest to crawl beneath a pile of debris to annoint a little girl who had been trapped for two days. The unfortunate girl had lain there throughout two successive night raids. The Priest was able only to reach through the rubble and touch her wrist but miraculously she was eventually dug out — alive.

Throughout those terrible days and nights the Priests were very brave, the people also had tremendous courage. One night during a bombing raid a Priest was hurrying along Marybone to an area where a high explosive bomb had fallen. The Priest found a woman lying in the road, her left leg had been severed. He knelt down beside the injured woman and tried to comfort her. She looked up, and with complete disregard for herself, she urged the Priest to hurry to Adlington Street where there were people badly hurt who needed him.

In other areas of Scotland Road and Great Homer Street, civil defence workers and wardens struggled on as each night produced more and more devastation and more casualties. Many of these brave rescue workers had been so hard pressed that they had been unable for days to remove their uniforms.

During the May 1941 blitz the residents of Scotland Road experienced many savage, sustained bombing attacks. Thursday 1st May saw the beginning of seven nights of hell. During that terrible week the German Luftwaffe dropped 2,000 high explosive bombs which destroyed or damaged thousands of homes. In one of the earlier raids the North Market in Cazneau Street was badly damaged.

May Blitz 1941. Scotland Road, between Mile End and Hornby Street, showing bomb crater at the top of Cazneau Street.

Saturday 2nd May and Sunday 3rd May 1941 was probably the most fearsome and destructive of all the raids. Many houses, schools and business premises in the area were blazing infernos, there were more than 400 recorded incidents. Between 10 o'clock on the Saturday night and five o'clock on the Sunday morning enemy bombers droned overhead releasing thousands of tons of high explosives and incendiaries on the city. Scotland Road had suffered German bombing in the previous December but had never experienced an onslaught such as this.

To combat the outbreaks of fires each street had organised its own little group of volunteer fire-fighters. They scaled ladders to the roof tops, used sand, water and stirrup pumps to quickly extinguish the numerous outbreak of flames. This gallant band of fire-fighters were constantly bedevilled by the horrific parachute mines which sailed overhead to land and explode in a great orange glow. One of these missiles fell into St. Gerard's Church, landed in a confessional box and burnt itself out.

High explosive bombs continued to fall, entire streets were flattened causing wreckage over a wide area. There were stables on fire in Newsham Street and William Moult Street. The local fire-fighters did tremendous work in getting the horses to safety and containing the outbreak of fire.

On 3rd May the Rotunda Theatre, Scotland Road's famous old landmark and place of entertainment was destroyed by enemy action. At the time part of the building was being used to store furniture from luxury Cunard liners which had been requisitioned as troopships. On the same night the Lyric Theatre at the bottom of Everton Valley, another famous old theatre, was destroyed.

During the air raids tram-cars and buses would stop at the nearest air raid shelter; air raid wardens and police blowing whistles, would order the passengers to take cover in the shelters.

On the Sunday morning following the raid the area presented a depressing sight. All sunlight was blacked out by a vast pall of smoke from the scores of buildings still burning. Hosepipes lay across the cobbled streets, police and rescue workers staggered on, tired and weary almost asleep on their feet, as the acrid smell of burning timber filled the air. Pavements were strewn with debris, roads and streets in Great Homer Street were impassable because of huge bomb craters; many were sealed off because of the danger from unexploded bombs. The water supply in the city had been cut off. This seriously hampered the efforts of the firemen who struggled to extinguish the numerous fires before darkness fell again. During the raids these firemen had worked at great risk because during their attempts to control the fires they were a continual target from enemy aircraft. There were many lives lost when a land mine made a direct hit on the tenements in Great Crosshall Street. Many families were buried and the situation was aggravated when fire broke out among the top layer of debris while rescuers were crawling beneath the shattered walls in an attempt to rescue the trapped and injured. Another block of tenements in Rose Hill was damaged and there were many people killed in Blackstock Gardens when a public shelter was hit. In later years open air Benediction was held on the site. Dozens of churches, shops and cinemas in the city were reduced to piles of rubble.

By the fourth night of the May blitz there had been enormous devastation. Each night there were hundreds of people from the Scotland Road district who left their homes and spent the night sleeping on the floor in the hall of Lord Derby's Estate.

During the Liverpool blitz many young 'Scottie Roaders' in the King's Regiment were stationed on the east coast. Night after night they listened as the German bombers droned overhead on their way to devastate Liverpool. The anti-aircraft guns would sometimes shoot down an enemy aircraft and as it came down in a sheet of flame one of the Liverpool lads in the unit would shout "One less for Scottie Road". There were a number of lads from the district in the anti-aircraft unit, they of course would be very concerned for their relatives at home particularly when the newscasters announced details the following morning of the previous nights air raids in the North West. Later some of the lads would be handed buff coloured envelopes which informed them of the tragic news. One young soldier arrived home to find an entire street flattened. He couldn't believe the devastation which had taken place in Candia Street and Mitylene Street. Another young soldier came home to learn that his young bride, of only a few months, had been killed during an air raid.

As the sirens sounded again on the night of 6th May 1941 the weary 'Scottie Roaders' prepared themselves for yet another sleepless night, another hammering from the German bombers. They all secretly wondered how much

longer they could continue. They did not know that their ordeal was almost over. At 4.30 a.m. on 8th May 1941 the 'all clear' sounded, and though no-one was aware of it at the time, it signalled the end of the May blitz. The Luftwaffe were never to return to torment Scotland Road on such a scale ever again.

There were many stories about the courage of the people of the district throughout those disastrous nights. But although destruction and death at times were all around them, the Germans failed to crush the indomitable spirit of the proud 'Scottie Roaders'.

In May 1941 a mass funeral was held in Anfield Cemetery when hundreds of victims of the bombings were buried in a common grave. To-day visitors to the grave see a long strip of green, framed in light grey stone. Alongside the grave there is a weeping elm tree. On a large memorial stone there is an inscription which tells that in the 170 feet long x 8 feet wide communal grave, lies the remains of 560 people who were killed during the Nazi raids on Liverpool. In this little tranquil part of Liverpool the remains lie side by side. It was impossible to say what creed the bodies were, the terrible mutilation made positive identification, in many cases, impossible. In that area of Anfield Cemetery lie the remains of many who were dug from the rubble and devastation of Great Homer Street and Scotland Road. The residents of this area of Liverpool paid a terrible price, entire families were wiped out, homes and possessions lost. Some people were never accounted for during that disastrous month of May 1941.

During the many raids on Scotland Road, there were many examples of the unique spirit and humour of the residents. During a raid people in the district had spent a long, dark, miserable night in an air raid shelter in Kew Street. The bombs had been exploding throughout the night and there were many surrounding buildings destroyed. As the enemy planes droned overhead, a little old lady seated in the corner nervously clutched her rosary beads. Suddenly there was a loud explosion which shook the foundation of the shelter and almost immediately after, stern voices were heard outside the shelter. The door of the shelter burst open and the people were ordered out of the shelter. The little old lady was first to come out and in the half light of the flames she could see two helmeted and masked figures approaching. She screamed out "Jesus, Mary and Joseph, the Germans are here, they've got us". What she had in fact seen and heard was not Germans in Kew Street but two air raid wardens who were evacuating the shelter because there was an incendiary bomb on the roof of the building.

Another example of the Scotland Road 'never say die' attitude was the 62 year old woman from Opie Street who was an air raid warden. When the bombs were falling and shrapnel whistling about she would be out on the street wearing her tin hat. When the German raiders passed overhead she would shake her fist at the planes and shout defiantly "Sod you! Sod you! You won't break us".

One warm evening during the war a young merchant seaman, home on leave, was kicking a football with some youngsters in Hook Street off Latimer Street. He was wearing a brilliant white shirt which he had bought during a previous 'trip' to New York. Suddenly a lone German raider came swooping down out of the clouds, machine guns blazing. Everyone scattered, the young man's mother came tearing out of the house yelling at him to get indoors with his white shirt because it was so white it was attracting the German planes. For the remainder of the evening his mother blamed him for almost getting them all killed by the Germans.

During the war, on the radio from Germany came the voice of 'Lord Haw-Haw' — William Joyce later executed for treason. His voice was recognised by the very distinct pronunciation of "Gaimany calling — Gaimany calling". On one occasion his propaganda claimed that the people of Great Homer Street were rioting and marching around the streets with 'white flags' and shouting for peace. During the May blitz, 'Lord Haw-Haw' claimed that there were people in Scotland Road who were flying 'white flags' from their chimney pots as a sign that they had 'had enough'. A young corporal returning from 48 hours leave in Great Homer Street was asked by his colleagues about the report of 'white flags' in 'Greaty' and 'Scottie', he reported that he had not seen any signs of surrender but he had seen a row of white chamber pots which had been strung together and hoisted to the roof of a block of tenements in Wilbraham Street. This, of course, was a typical 'Scottie Road' response to 'Lord Haw-Haw's' propaganda.

One of the unsung heroes of the blitz in Scotland Road was 18yrs old James Coultard, a scout ambulance messenger. He was an altar boy in St. Alphonsus Church, Great Mersey Street and during the nights of the blitz, he was at the A.R.P. Control Centre at St. Joseph's, Rose Hill. He and other scouts acted as guides to the ambulance drivers who were sometimes strangers to the area and not familiar with the tiny back-alleys of Great Homer Street. His knowledge of the area was of great assistance to the ambulance drivers who would have to find their way through blacked-out streets to some terrible incidents. On the night of Saturday 2nd May 1941, Jimmy was doing his stint of fire-watching on the roof of St. Alphonsus. At about midnight that night, Scotland Road was under heavy attack. He spotted a parachute mine which landed on the roof of a row of houses in Great Mersey Street and exploded. He dashed down the stairs and headed towards where the mine had exploded. The house had been reduced to a heap of rubble. It was the house of his young friend Peter who had left him only a few minutes earlier to see if his family were alright. Jimmy never saw his pal alive again.

Jimmy made desperate attempts to release some people who were trapped in the debris which was on fire. There was a young woman pinned beneath a gas stove. He crawled through a hole between falling rafters and managed to free her. He was so exhausted that he had to be dragged out by the other rescuers. After a brief rest he insisted on getting involved again and crawled in with water to those people who were trapped. He was awarded the George Medal. His award citation stated that he had succeeded in locating the position of the trapped people and it was largely due to his individual effort that they were rescued.

Conway Street between 1941-42.
Tiny back-to-back houses destroyed by enemy action.

BLITZ CASUALTIES LIVERPOOL		
	Killed	Seriously Injured
August 1940	37	73
September 1940	221	357
October 1940	106	90
November 1940	305	192
December 1940	412	382
January 1941	43	23
February 1941	2	8
March 1941	101	99
April 1941	36	104
May 1941	1453	1065

After a weary sleepless night, dawn approached and brought the welcoming sound of the "all clear". Many people returned in the chill morning air to find their homes destroyed by enemy action. This was the heartbreaking sight which met the residents of Virgil Street in May 1941.

Celebrities and Personalities

Not all the great men and women of Liverpool have come from the more polished areas. From the heart of Scotland Road have come some of the city's best men and women. There have been Members of Parliament, Local Politicians, International Entertainers, Professional Boxers, Professional Footballers and so on. All have distinguished themselves in their chosen profession and no matter where they have gone in connection with their career, they have been a credit to Scotland Road.

CILLA BLACK

One of Scotland Road's famous daughters is Cilla Black, the talented, international pop singer. In February 1964 her second record, 'Anyone Who Had A Heart', rocketed to the top of the charts in ten days.

Cilla was born Cilla Marie White on 27th May 1943 and grew up in the family home above Murray's Barber Shop at 380 Scotland Road. She had three brothers — George, John and Allen, who together with Mum and Dad, were a very close-knit happy family. Living on a busy main road it was impossible for the youngsters to play out. This was a constant problem for all the mothers with young children in the area. When Cilla was three years old she went to nursery school at St. Mary's, Great Crosshall Street. Her mother took her there and back every day on the tram-car. When Cilla was five years old she attended St. Anthony's school in Newsham Street where she was to remain for the rest of her school days.

She enjoyed every minute of her time at St. Anthony's. Her Headmistress was Sister Marie Julie, who although she was a very strict disciplinarian, was beloved

by all her pupils. Cilla's best friend at school was Patti Singleton who lived in Newsham Street and who was a practical joker just like Cilla. Together they were involved in many hilarious situations at school. One of Cilla's best loved treats when she was a little girl was to be taken by her Dad to the pictures in town. When they came out of the cinema they would go and have a meal in Woolworths.

When Cilla was about ten years old she was a member of a 'gang' of five girls all in the same class at St. Anthony's. After school it was the practice of many of the children to go to the play-centre in Penrhyn Street school and it was here that Cilla's singing talent developed. There was a singing contest each evening and the first prize was threepence. Cilla entered these contest and won almost every evening. The teachers thought that Cilla had an unfair advantage because all her school pals came along to support her. So to try and ensure that the contest was 'fair' to everyone, the teachers insisted that all the contestants would use numbers instead of their names. In spite of this Cilla still won on the strength of her singing talent.

In her early teens Cilla and her friends became very involved in pop music, their favourite was Frankie Lymon and the Teenagers, the popular American singing group. In order to identify with the singing group 'Cilla's Gang' all bought pairs of blue jeans from a Mail Order Catalogue for 1/3d per week.

At school Cilla did very well in her school work, she always finished in the top three in her examinations and received very good reports. One of the things that Cilla remembers at school was the day she broke her nose. Sister Marie Julie took charge of the situation and proceeded to put a large bunch of cold keys down Cilla's back in an attempt to stop the blood pouring from her nose.

When Cilla was fifteen she left her beloved St. Anthony's and went to Anfield Commercial College to study shorthand typing. Later she was employed by B.I.C.C. as a dictaphone typist at their offices in Liverpool.

In 1963 she made her first record, a Lennon/McCartney composition called 'Love of the Loved' and she was suddenly on her way to stardom. She became an international star in a glittering world far removed from the cobbled streets of Great Homer Street. But no matter how much Cilla's life has changed since her days in the classroom of St. Anthony's she will always love 'Scottie Road'. Her advice to youngsters embarking on a career in show-business, "Don't ever forget your humble beginnings, wherever you go, always remember your parents and the home that made everything possible".

ALDERMAN DAVID COWLEY

David Cowley was the boy from the back streets of Scotland Road who grew up to become Lord Mayor of Liverpool and have a very distinguished career in public life.

David was the youngest of several children and was only one year old when his father died. The family home was near the Rotunda and David went to St. Anthony's school. He developed an interest in politics at an early age as a consequence of the influence of his stepfather Charles Butwell, who at the time was a senior official in the local Transport & General Workers Union, and who encouraged David to participate in local political activities.

When David left school he was employed as an apprentice butcher in a shop in Anfield. His brother, Alexander, was killed at the beginning of the second world war and David, then 16, left his job to enlist in the Merchant Navy. He joined Alfred Holt & Company as a deckboy on the s.s. Atreus. In 1941 he was a member of the crew of the s.s. Eumaeus when she was torpedoed off the West Coast of Africa. After 14 hours adrift at sea he was picked up by an Indian destroyer. His family had been informed that he was 'missing presumed killed'. They were overjoyed when they received the information that David was one of the survivors.

After leaving the Merchant Navy in 1946 he became a dredgerman with the Mersey Docks & Harbour Board for three years and in 1949 he took control of the family tobacco business in Scotland Road. The little shop was on the corner of Taylor Street.

He was elected to the City Council in 1951 as the member for South Scotland Ward and was appointed an Alderman in 1959. He became Lord Mayor in 1965 and although he was the city's youngest ever Lord Mayor at 41 he was to be particularly outstanding in this role. He made new friends wherever he went and did a tremendous amount of work to project a favourable image for the city.

One of the highlights of Alderman Cowley's year as Lord Mayor was Everton's return from their 1966 F.A. Cup triumph over Sheffield Wednesday at Wembley.

ROBERT PARRY, M.P.

The grubby little youngster who played on the bombed sites in Scotland Road now sits in the House of Commons as a member for Exchange Division of Liverpool. Bob has spent his entire life in the Scotland Road area. He was born in Christian Street and when he was five years old his family moved to Gerard Crescent. He was baptised in the old Holy Cross Church in Great Crosshall Street and attended Bishop Goss school.

Employed in the building trade, Bob became an activist in the Labour Party and Trade Union movement. He was elected to the Liverpool Trades Council at the age of 19. He was a member of the Liverpool City Council, representing St. James Ward and at the same time he was the Chairman of the Exchange Division Labour Party. Later he became a full time Trade Union Organiser.

He was elected to the House of Commons in 1970, at that time he was 37 years old and was the youngest Member of Parliament on Merseyside. As the elected member for Exchange Division he is representing in Parliament the people he was born and reared with. He still lives with his family in a little corporation flat in Vauxhall Gardens in the same environment in which he was born.

DAVID LOGAN, M.P.

David Logan, the well known Member of Parliament for the Scotland Division, was born in the area and lived all his life at the top of Kew Street. He represented the Scotland Division for 33 years and was still an active Member of Parliament in 1962 at the age of 90. He died some years later and is buried in Ford Cemetery.

'DANDY' PAT BYRNE

'Dandy' Patrick Byrne was the licencee of the old 'Morning Star' in Scotland Place. It was here that Irish leader De Valera hid, when he escaped from gaol, before boarding a ship to America.

'Dandy' Pat was noted for his generosity to poor people, no poor person was ever turned away empty handed by him. A memorial — the Byrne Fountain in polished granite was erected by his customers. He died on 8th May 1890 and is buried at Co Wexford.

He was a City Councillor who was distinguished for his services to the ratepayers and benefaction to the poor of the district. He was called 'Dandy' Pat because he was always immaculately dressed in a seal skin vest and white topper. To-day the Byrne Fountain is erected in Standish Street near Marybone.

SETH DAVEY

About the year 1900 an old coloured gentleman named Seth Davey used to sit near the corner of Bevington Bush and entertain the local children with his dancing dolls. He was very popular with children and would sing negro songs and tell them stories about his days as a slave.

He would have his little dolls dancing on a board and in the evening he would take the board and his colourful dolls into Lee's bootshop facing 'Paddy's Market' and leave them there overnight.

In November 1968 a song based on the legend of Seth Davey won a gold disc in Australia and was top of the charts in Ireland. Some of the words from the song were:— 'Drinking buttermilk all the week, and whisky on a Sunday'.

Murder : Mystery : Money Forgers

The Skirving Street Poisoners : The Skeleton in the Cylinder : The Virgil Street Forgers :
Spring-Heeled Jack.

THE SKIRVING STREET POISONERS

Scotland Road 1880, with its inhabitants suffering harsh poverty which hopefully we will never experience again, was one of the poorest areas in Liverpool. The side streets of this famous road were the setting for this wicked story. It is a story of murder, of four innocent people who became the victims of two greedy Victorian women — Catherine Flanagan aged 50 and her sister, Margaret Higgins aged 39. They were both widows, both drunken suspect characters whose devotion to the bottle was not restricted to alcohol but extended to the poison bottle.

In November 1880 the sisters were the occupants of a house in Skirving Street, a little cobbled street inhabited by working class people. Also living in the house were five other people. They were John Flanagan, the 22 years old son of widow Flanagan. A lodger by the name of Thomas Higgins who later married Margaret Higgins (at that time widow Thompson). Mary Higgins the 8 year old daughter of Thomas Higgins. Another lodger, Patrick Jennings and his 16 year old daughter Margaret. During the next three years these people were to vanish from the scene one by one. The only survivor was Patrick Jennings.

The first victim was young John Flanagan; he died on 7th December 1880. His mother overcome with grief at the loss of her son, collected the Burial Fund money, about £70.

In the old days, before the introduction of the welfare state, the poor people, no matter how desperately poor they lived, felt it a matter of pride to have a decent funeral. This was provided for by weekly contributions to a Burial Club. To the people of the slums, these Burial Clubs were a means of ensuring dignity in death which was certainly something which they had been denied throughout their struggling lifetime.

The two sisters realised that if you were to take out Insurances with a number of Insurance Clubs and the person nominated on those policies obligingly died, there could be a considerable amount of money due to the benefactor. With this in mind the sisters had laid their plans.

In 1881 Margaret married her second husband — Thomas Higgins the lodger, who worked as a bricklayer. In November 1882 the sudden death occured of little Mary Higgins, there were tears as her stepmother wasted little time in drawing the Insurance money.

In January 1883, only two months after the death of Mary Higgins, another member of the household was dead — Margaret Jennings. As in the previous cases one of the sisters reached out to obtain the Insurance money even before the funeral took place.

The ghoulish sisters reviewed their position; it appeared to be very satisfactory. They had obtained a considerable amount of money and financially their murderous deeds had been profitable. There had been no mistakes and as far as they knew, no one suspected anything.

But there had been three deaths in one house in a very short space of time, it could start people talking and lead to unwanted investigations. They decided to call a temporary halt to their murderous activities and move from the house in Skirving Street. They, and the remaining members of the household, moved across Scotland Road to 105 Latimer Street. They settled down and for the next three months, lived their lives quite normally, the neighbours suspecting nothing sinister about the sisters. Then in October 1883 they moved house again. This time to 27 Ascot Street which was in fact just around the corner from Latimer Street. It was here that the sisters looked for another victim. They selected the unfortunate Thomas Higgins and promptly took out a number of Insurance policies on his life. The familiar well rehearsed pattern of murder was in operation again.

Four weeks later, in November 1883, Thomas Higgins suddenly became ill. He appeared to be in terrible pain and moaned throughout the night. The following day he was dead. The doctor who examined the body certified death was due to excessive drinking.

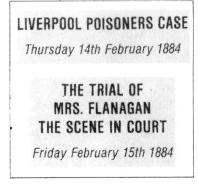

LIVERPOOL POISONERS CASE

Thursday 14th February 1884

THE TRIAL OF
MRS. FLANAGAN
THE SCENE IN COURT

Friday February 15th 1884

The Headlines as the case was reported in the 'Liverpool Echo' in February 1884.

But it was at this point that things began to go sour for the sisters, they had been involved in their last murder undertaking. Their last victim, Thomas Higgins, had a brother, Patrick Higgins, who had discovered that the life of the deceased had been insured with no less than six different companies. He was more than suspicious and alerted the police and the doctor. The coroners office became involved and moved quickly.

On the day of the funeral the horse drawn hearse stood in the road-way outside the house in Ascot Street, the Undertaker inside the house making final arrangements before the body of Thomas Higgins was removed for burial. In the back kitchen there was the sound of drunken laughter and the clinking of beer glasses — there did not appear to be much grief in the house.

Suddenly two strangers entered the house and after a brief word with the Undertaker they were directed to widow Higgins. One of the gentlemen identified himself as being from the coroner's office and his colleague was a doctor. They explained quietly that the funeral could not take place that day and that further enquiries were to be made. A post-mortem was ordered and the following week the bodies of John Flanagan, Mary Higgins and Margaret Jennings were exhumed. The experts discovered traces of arsenic in all three cases.

Margaret Higgins and Catherine Flanagan were arrested and subsequently charged with murder. During the ensuing police investigations further evidence was unearthed in the cellar in Ascot Street. A mug, a bottle and a spoon were found, all bore traces of arsenic. In addition some of the clothing which the women were wearing at the time of their arrest yielded evidence of arsenic.

In the trial that followed in February 1884 the prosecution evidence was that the sisters had obtained the arsenic by soaking household fly-papers in water, the poisonous water being preserved and later administered to the unsuspecting victims.

The trial lasted three days and after considering the evidence, the jury found both prisoners guilty of the murders. During a snowstorm on the morning of 3rd March 1884, in the old Kirkdale Gaol, the two sisters were executed.

THE SKELETON IN THE CYLINDER

A group of young children had been playing happily on a blitzed site at the junction of Fulford Street and Great Homer Street. It was a bright sunny day in July 1945.

Amongst the bricks and rubble on the bombed site, there lay a mysterious black iron cylinder about seven feet long and eighteen inches in diameter. As one of the young boys crouched behind it he saw a boot protruding from the flattened edges of the open end of the cylinder. The boy summoned the rest of his playmates. One of the more venturesome children bent down and eased the boot from the narrow opening. There were gasps of horror, for as the children watched fascinated, they saw the boot released to reveal human bones inside the dark cylinder.

The children were white-faced. One of the older boys ran as fast as he could to report the gruesome discovery to the policeman on point-duty at the busy junction of Scotland Road and Kirkdale Road. The boy breathlessly poured out his story of the cylinder on the blitzed site and urged the policeman to come back with him. It was Friday 13th July and the policeman quietly muttered something about it being "Friday 13th" and followed the excited boy back to where the cylinder lay. He bent down and looked through the narrow gap in the top of the cylinder.

Shortly afterwards a van arrived at the site. The cylinder was loaded and quickly driven away to the city mortuary. Later that afternoon, officials stood in silence as the cylinder was carefully cut open by an engineer. When the top of the cylinder was lifted off, the observers saw a very weird sight.

There, lying upon a rough layer of dusty decayed sacking, was the body of a man dressed in tattered Victorian clothing. He was wearing a black morning coat with cloth covered buttons, black waistcoat, narrow striped trousers, cream shirt, black bow tie and the elastic sided old fashioned boots.

A post-mortem examination was conducted on the remains by Dr. C. Harrison, a Pathologist at Liverpool University. Later, when disclosing his findings, Dr. Harrison commented that it had been the most extraordinary post-mortem examination he had ever undertaken. It was revealed that the remains were those of a male, the bones indicating that he was more that 25 years of age but since his teeth were well preserved and the hair adhering to the scull was

**SKELETON IN THE CYLINDER
BOYS FIND ON
BLITZ SITE**

Friday 13th July 1945

**CITY C.I.D. PROBE
CYLINDER RIDDLE
COMB RECORDS FOR
MISSING**

Saturday 14th July 1945

**INQUEST ON SKELETON
LIVERPOOL MYSTERY
UNSOLVED**

Thursday 19th July 1945

The Headlines as the case was reported in the 'Liverpool Echo' in July 1945.

brown and had not turned grey, he was probably middle aged and about six feet in height. There was no way of establishing how he had died but he had been dead for many years.

From there on the case was referred to the Liverpool City Police for further investigation. It was thought, at first, that the body was that of someone who had crawled into the cylinder during the war, to seek protection from the bombings, and had been killed. It was also suggested that the remains were that of a murder victim. Local Detectives were unable to solve the problem and the assistance of the Forensic Science Laboratory at Preston was enlisted. The renowned forensic expert Dr. J.B. Firth came to Liverpool and took possession of all the available evidence including clothing and a number of other clues — a gold signet ring, hall-marked London 1859, a penknife, a handkerchief and a pocket diary for the year 1885. There were also some papers which had been in the lining of the coat, time had reduced the wad of papers into a solid mass of wax rendering them inseparable and illegible.

But the experts at the Forensic Laboratories were able to treat the documents with chemicals and solvents and eventually those papers were readable.

The painstaking exercise had proved worthwhile, the papers contained vital clues. Among the documents were some letterheads for the firm of T.C. Williams & Co of Leeds Street, Liverpool. Also included was a personal document addressed to Mr. T. C. Williams. In spite of searching tests the experts were unable to detect any evidence of poison in the remains to account for the death. However they did estimate that the death had occurred about July 1885. The case was inconclusive and was referred back to the Liverpool C.I.D. for investigation.

A Senior Officer was assigned the task of solving the remainder of the mystery. After thoroughly searching through many old Liverpool Trade Directories it was established that in 1883 there had been a firm of oil and varnish merchants named T.C. Williams & Co. in business at 20 Leeds Street. It was also established that the owner of the company was a Mr. Thomas Creegan Williams living in Clifton Road, Anfield. He was born in 1830 and began his working life as a salesman but eventually set up his own business. He married a Miss Elizabeth Lea and there was one child from the marriage — a son, Thomas Lea Creegan Williams. Elizabeth Williams died in May 1878 and was buried at Anfield Cemetery.

Further investigations into the firm of T.C. Williams uncovered the fact that in 1884 the principal of the company was being examined by a firm of accountants in connection with bankruptcy. It was there that the clues ended. There was no official entry of bankruptcy and more significant, there was no further evidence of the existence of the firm of T.C. Williams in any Trade Directories after 1884. Neither was there any record of the death of Thomas Creegan Williams.

In August 1945 the coroner officially recorded an open verdict on the death of an unknown man. But unofficially, having regard to the evidence available, it would seem probable that the remains in the cylinder were those of Thomas Creegan Williams.

During the police investigations an 80 year old man, who had once lived in Leeds Street, came forward to make a very interesting statement. He said that when he was a boy he used to tease Mr. Williams in his shop by ringing the old fashioned bells behind the door by opening and closing the door. On one occasion Mr. Williams caught the boy and hit him about the head. It was during this chastisement that the boy saw and felt the blood stone signet ring.

Almost forty years after the discovery of the skeleton in the cylinder we do not know for certain how Williams — presuming of course that it was Williams — came to be in the cylinder in Great Homer Street. There were a number of theories advanced at the time:—

1, He could have committed suicide.

2. He may have been a murder victim, by some means, which left no traceable evidence at post-mortem.

3. He may have been running away from his creditors and crawled into the cylinder to sleep, shut off the air and asphyxiated himself.

But for whatever the reason, the cylinder retained its secret for over sixty years and even today the mystery of the skeleton in the cylinder, officially remains unsolved.

SPRING-HEELED JACK

It was a day in September 1904 that the startled residents of Great Homer Street saw the Leaping Man. Hundreds of people stood and watched in fascinated fear as Spring-Healed Jack hopped up and down William Henry Street. He made colossal leaps — some people who witnessed the spectacle claimed the creature jumped more than twenty five feet from the sidewalk to the rooftops.

Terrified women quickly ordered their children into the safety of their homes where they remained trembling with fright. The men, trying to demonstrate their bravery, stood in groups and pointed at the amazing sight. There were hundreds of people in the district who saw the weird creature. This unbelievable exhibition continued for about fifteen minutes until 'Jack' finally leaped clean over the houses from Stitt Street into Haigh Street then leapt back again over the rooftops down William Henry Street into Soho Street where he vanished out of sight.

The appearance of Spring-Heeled Jack was no isolated incident. Reports of his acitivities had been circulating in many parts of Britain for many years. There were tales of the mysterious 'Jumping Man' having been sighted on the outskirts of London. It was claimed that he came bounding out of the darkness of a cemetery and almost scared the local people to death. The police in the area were ordered by the Lord Mayor of London to hold an investigation. During the course of these enquiries the police interviewed a 25 year old young woman who lived in an isolated house in the East End of London. She related how on a dark winter's night there had come a violent banging on the front-door of the house. When she opened the door she was confronted by a man in a long black cloak. Standing there he suddenly flung back the cloak to reveal an abnormally thin body covered in a tight fitting white rubber type garment. He stood glaring through burning red eyes; the girl was petrified. He lunged forward, great spurts of white flame pouring from his mouth. The girl screamed, her family came running to her assistance. The amazing creature, with one tremendous leap, vanished into the darkness.

During the 1890's it was rumoured that Spring-Heeled Jack had been sighted in Liverpool on a number of occasions. He is said to have been seen on the top of the reservoir in High Park Street, he was also seen in the vicinity of Childwall Abbey. A youngster claimed to have seen him crouched on the steeple of a church in Shaw Street.

To return to the excitement in William Henry Street in 1904, 'Jack' bounded around in Soho Street causing tremendous commotion. Then suddenly, with one final leap over the rooftops, he was gone . . . never to return. Spring-Heeled Jack had taken his last leap into the legends of history leaving a mystery which remains as deep today as it was in 1904.

COUNTERFEITORS OF VIRGIL STREET

In the early 1800's when Virgil Street was lined with the houses of wealthy merchants there was a family of very clever couterfeitors in their midst.

For some time the Royal Mint had been investigating the flood of forged five shilling pieces circulating throughout the country. In spite of intense enquiries there did not appear to be any clues to establish the source of origin of the forged money.

But the point that really baffled the authorities was that each forged coin contained genuine silver, the quantity of each coin being valued at about four shillings. Why would anyone use real silver to manufacture forged coins?

A detailed examination of the counterfeit coins revealed that they could only have been made by people possessing a high degree of skill and expensive equipment. It was evident also that the forgers must be involved in receiving stolen silver plate. It would not have been practical for them to have continued to purchase silver at the market price.

This assumption was subsequently proved correct. About this time a large-scale robbery of silver plate took place in Liverpool, attracting the attention of the investigators in the city. Soon after there were a lot of enquiries made which led the investigators to a large house in Virgil Street, off Great Homer Street. Here lived a very wealthy and respected family. There was a very attractive daughter named Julia, who was admired by all her friends and neighbours for her lady-like appearance and excellent manners.

The two officers working on the case had tried unsuccessfully to enter the house on various pretexts. Eventually one of them, disguised as a postman, boldly approached the house and knocked on the door. The door was opened by Julia and before she could prevent them, the 'postman' together with his colleague, were in the house. They discovered a considerable amount of stolen silver plate, a hoard of forged coins and some very expensive machinery for producing them.

The owner of the house, a shop keeper, was not involved in the crime but Julia and her brother were arrested. They were both subsequently tried and convicted. They were transported to Australia as a punishment.

Usually that would be the end of such a case where the prisoners were transported but it was not so in this particular instance. About a year later Mr. Power, solicitor for the Royal Mint who had led the prosecution against the forgers, received a letter from Julia. She informed him that when she had first been transported she had cursed him for his part in her conviction. But now she praised him for having her transported. She described how she had married a wealthy man and had a beautiful home in Sydney; she concluded that she was very happy and it was all due to him.

Virgil Street, off Great Homer Street, about the time of the counterfeiting.

'Scottie' Soccer Stars

The schools from the Scotland Road area enjoyed an excellent reputation for sporting achievements. They won many trophies for football against other schools in the city. This was something of an achievement when one considers the deprived home backgrounds of most of the lads. The people in the district were 'football mad' and almost as soon as a boy could walk he was learning to dribble and shoot. The lads lived for the game of football and would be kicking or heading a ball against a wall at every opportunity. Some of the best footballers ever to grace the game were born and brought up in the side streets of Scotland Road.

Football was played in the cobbled streets with coats on the ground to mark the goals. The nearest grass pitches were at Stanley Park, Long Lane and Walton Hall Avenue; all were a tram-ride away and not many of the lads could afford the fare to make the journey. There was an area where football was played. This was situated near the canal and was known locally as the 'Lock-fields'. After the war years the games were played on the blitzed sites. These areas were covered with black cinder gravel which caused many cuts to the players' hands and knees. It was a very rough playing surface but none of the lads ever complained, even when some of them had gravel stones so deeply embedded in their hands that they had to attend hospital to have the stones extracted and the wound dressed. Two of the most popular 'cinder' pitches in Great Homer Street were Arkwright Street and Christ Church. There were always matches being played on these sites, very often there were as many as sixteen players on each side.

ST. ANTHONY'S WINNERS CATHOLIC SCHOOLS CUP AND SHIELD 1919-1920

All the Catholic schools in the area played in the Catholic Cup Competition and from the year of its inception — 1900 — many school teams from Scotland Road won the coveted trophy. There was a great friendly rivalry between the schools, each team enjoying a tremendous following wherever they played. The supporters would parade around the parish with the cups and shield, the players of the winning team being carried shoulder high by their football crazy supporters. In May 1950 when St. Anthony's defeated St. Teresa's in the Catholic Cup Final, the entire team was carried on the shoulders of their supporters from Anfield all the way back to Newsham Street. The captain of the team, Peter Weir, proudly holding the Cup aloft, was carried on the shoulders of a well known character, Henry Smith. Henry himself had been an outstanding player in his youth and had played in the St. Anthony's Cup and Shield winning team of 1920. The cheers were tremendous as the crowds lined Scotland Road and applauded the team.

The carnival atmosphere continued late into the evening as the happy supporters danced their way around the streets of the parish. They waved their banners — the famous Black and Amber colours of St. Anthony's and sang the traditional football battle hymns:—

> *'It's a grand old team to play for*
> *It's a team that's sure to win*
> *Have you ever heard their history*
> *It's enough to make your heart go*
> *Rah . . . Rah . . . Rah . . . Rah*
> *We don't care if we win or lose or draw*
> *We don't have to care*
> *All we know is there's going to be a match*
> *And all ST. ANTHONY'S will be there.'*

C. Cup Winners — Teams from the Scotland Road area.

Season	Cup Winners
1902-03	St. Alban's
1903-04	St. Alban's
1904-05	St. Sylvester's
1906-07	Bishop Goss
1908-09	St. Alban's
1913-14	St. Mary's Highfield Street
1919-20	St. Anthony's
1921-22	St. Sylvester's
1926-27	St. Sylvester's
1929-30	Our Lady Immaculate's
1930-31	St. Anthony's
1932-33	St. Sylvester's
1933-34	St. Sylvester's
1947-48	St. Sylvester's
1949-50	St. Anthony's
1950-51	St. Sylvester's
1951-52	St. Anthony's
1953-54	St. Sylvester's
1960-61	St. Gregory's
1964-65	Archbishop Whiteside
1971-72	St. Gregory's

St. Sylvester's League Champions 1931-32.

The two most successful schools in the district were ancient rivals St. Anthony's and St. Sylvester's. The rivalry was so intense because the two schools and parishes were adjacent with many boys living in St. Sylvester's parish and attending St. Anthony's school and vice-versa. The sporting traditions of both schools extended back to the origin of the Catholic Schools' League.

Mr. J.P. Callaghan, the former Headmaster of St. Sylvester's school, was the President of the Liverpool Catholic Schools' Athletic Association from 1899 until 1939, the Association controlled Catholic Schools' Football. In 1931, when schools' football came under the control of the Liverpool Schools' Football Association, the first chairman was Mr. J.C. Murray, Headmaster of St. Anthony's, whilst the Secretary was from St. Sylvester's. Both the schools have therefore played very important roles in the development of Schools' football in Liverpool.

The most memorable Catholic Cup Final in the history of the competition was one that generations of Scotland Road people had waited for — St. Anthony's versus St. Sylvester's. The game was played at Anfield in May 1951 before a crowd of almost 9,000. This must surely be a record attendance for an inter-schools game.

The schools in the district supplied a steady stream of players to the Liverpool Boys' team. Every season there were representatives from the area but one particular season — 1953-54, one of the occasions when they won the English Schools' Trophy — there were no less than six lads from Scotland Road in the team:— T. Gannon (All Souls), S. Roach (St. Sylvester's), F. McGowan (Our Lady's, Titchfield), J. Harrison (St. Anthony's), G. Sinnott (All Souls), J. Morrissey (St. Sylvester's).

In season 1952-53 St. Anthony's provided three players for the Liverpool Boys' team:— J. Melia, C. Phillips, T. Johnson.

St. Anthony's Junior Cup Winners 1948.
Back Row, Left to Right:—
Carberry, Johnson, Weir, Boland, Groves, O'Connel, Manning.
Front Row Left to Right:—
Molyneux, Campbell, O'Connor, Smith, Kehoe.

Boys from schools in the Scotland Road district who played for Liverpool Boys in **Competition** matches from 1945 to 1981.

Season	Name	School
1945/46	A. Downes	St. Sylvester's
	J. Crighton	St. Sylvester's
	T. Kenny	St. Sylvester's
	M. McDermott	St. Sylvester's
1947/48	G. Tansy	St. Sylvester's
1948/49	G. Tansy	St. Sylvester's
	J. Broderick	St. Sylvester's
1949/50	C. Murphy	Major Street
	M. Joyce	Titchfield St.
	P. Weir	St. Anthony's
1950/51	E. Smith	Titchfield St.
	G. Morrison	St. Anthony's
	J. Moody	St. Augustine's
1951/52	R. Campbell	St. Anthony's
	J. Melia	St. Anthony's
	E. Holmes	Titchfield St.
	E. Corcoran	Major Street
1952/53	J. Melia	St. Anthony's
	T. Johnson	St. Anthony's
	C. Phillips	St. Anthony's

Catholic Schools' Cup — FINAL

ST. SYLVESTER'S v. ST. ANTHONY'S

KICK-OFF 7-30 P.M.

Also Junior Catholic Schools' League Final at 6-0 p.m.

At LIVERPOOL F.C. GROUND

(By kind permission of the Directors)

On THURSDAY, MAY 17th, 1951

ST. SYLVESTER'S
(Red)

RIGHT   LEFT

(1)
J. McNALLY

(2)   (3)
A. CLINTON   J. McEVOY

(4)   (5)   (6)
J. WESTHOFF   S. BRODERICK   J. KELLY

(7)   (8)   (9)   (10)   (11)
J. SMITH   C. BRENNAN   J. ROSSITER   J. STEPHENS   S. McDONALD
(Captain)   *Reserve—G. Doyle.*

A. CORKE   F. LAMBE   L. CARBERRY   J. KEARNS   E. McNALLY
(11)   (10)   (9)   (8)   (7)

J. BEATTIE   G. MORRISON (Captain)   R. CAMPBELL
(6)   (5)   (4)

B. KELLY   J. DYER
(3)   (2)

T. POWER

(1)

LEFT   *(Black & Amber)*   RIGHT

Reserve—G. White.   ST. ANTHONY'S

Referee: Mr. N. McWADE.
Linesmen: Mr. M. COLEMAN and Mr. C. BULLEN

PROGRAMME - - - 1d.

TWO MATCHES YOU MUST NOT MISS!

Lancashire Schools' Cup Final — 2nd Leg.
LIVERPOOL BOYS v. MANCHESTER BOYS
Saturday next, May 19th, at Anfield - - - Kick-off 10-45 a.m.

— AND —

English Schools' Trophy Final 2nd Leg.
LIVERPOOL BOYS v. BRIERLEY HILL BOYS
Wednesday next, May 23rd at Goodison Park - Kick-off 7-0 p.m.

Opposite:
This was the programme for the inter-schools match at Liverpool F.C. ground, when almost 9,000 people turned out to watch a Cup Final between two teams from Scotland Road.

St. Anthony's 1950-51.
Cup Finalists.

Back Row — Left to Right:—
J. Kearns, J. Cannon, G. White, T. Power, S. McCann, R. Campbell, J. Melia, E. McNally.

Front Row — Left to Right:—
F. Lamb, L. Carberry, G. Morrison, J. Dyer, T. Corke.

Three of the lads in this team went on to become outstanding professional footballers:- R. Campbell (Liverpool, Portsmouth), J. Melia (Liverpool, Wolverhampton Wanderers, Southampton), L. Carberry (Ipswich Town).

1953/54	T. Gannon	All Souls
	F. McGowan	Titchfield St.
	J. Harrison	St. Anthony's
	J. Morrissey	St. Sylvester's
	S. Roach	St. Sylvester's
	G. Sinnott	All Souls
1954/55	J. Nesbit	St. Sylvester's
	J. Morrissey	St. Sylvester's
1955/56	T. Atkinson	Major Street
1957/58	M. Gannon	All Souls
	B. Murphy	Titchfield St.
1962/63	W. Baker	Roscommon St.
1964/65	C. Dunleavey	St. Gregory's
	E. Card	Roscommon St.
1965/66	J. Bowman	St. Gregory's
	W. Miller	St. Gregory's
	P. Duffy	St. Pius X
	J. Lundon	St. Pius X
1966/67	W. Kenny	Archbishop Whiteside
	J. Muscatelli	St. Gregory's
1967/68	J. Smith	St. Gregory's
	A. Moorecroft	St. Gregory's
	J. Moran	Archbishop Whiteside
	F. Corrigan	St. Pius X
1970/71	H. Charalambous	Roscommon St.
1972/73	S. Vaughan	St. Gregory's
1973/74	J. Carrol	St. Pius X
1975/76	D. Corrigan	St. Pius X
1976/77	S. Furlong	St. Gregory's
	D. Watson	St. Pius X

SCHOOLBOY INTERNATIONALS

1951	J. Keeley	Our Lady Immaculate
1952	J. Keeley	Our Lady Immaculate
1953	J. Melia	St. Anthony's
1955	J. Morrissey	St. Sylvester's
1963	J. Baker	Roscommon St.
1967	W. Kenny	Archbishop Whiteside
1968	J. Smith	St. Gregory's

There were many players in the district who went on to become professional footballers most of them beginning their career with either Everton or Liverpool. A number of these lads were exceptionally outstanding and distinguished themselves in the game winning many honours. Some of them have since become successful Managers with First Division Clubs.

JIMMY MELIA

Born in Penrhyn Street in 1937, attended St. Anthony's school. At 12 years old he was showing glimpses of his genius on the blitzed site behind Wilbraham House. A member of the school's first team he was selected for Liverpool Schoolboys and was a sensation. In addition to his tremendous dribbling abilities he had the knack of streaking though gaps in the defence and scoring goals. On one occasion during a Liverpool Boys game at Penny Lane he scored four goals in the first fourteen minutes. After some brilliant games for the City team he was selected to play for England Boys' against Eire at Portsmouth in 1953. He played alongside Bobby Charlton but neither of them realised that ten years later they would form the England left wing against Scotland as full Internationals.

Jimmy joined Liverpool's ground staff straight from school at 15. People who knew him as a youngster were surprised that he joined Liverpool because he was always an 'Evertonian'. He played in the Liverpool Reserve team under the guidance of Bob Paisley, who was then responsible for the youngsters on the books. He signed as a professional at 17. He played for England Youth against Denmark and Holland. It was after such a Youth International game in 1955, that Don Welsh, then Manager at Anfield, told Jimmy that he was to make his senior debut against Nottingham Forest at Anfield the following Saturday. Liverpool won 5-2 and Jimmy scored on his debut.

He was soon established as a permanent member of the first team and continued to delight the 'Kop' with his individual skills. He reached his peak as a professional player during Liverpool's Second Division Championship year in 1961-62. He was rewarded with full International honours.

He moved from Liverpool to Wolves in March '65 for £50,000 and remained at Molyneux for a year. He was transferred to Southampton for £40,000 and led the team to the Second Division Championship in 1967. In 1969 he joined Aldershot as a player/manager and did some tremendous work for the club. During his playing career he played in 600 league games and scored 110 goals.

In 1972 he was appointed Manager of Crewe Alexandre and in 1975 was Manager of Southport for a brief period. He was appointed Manager of a Middle East team — Als Haab. In 1977 he went out to California to coach California Lasers in the American Soccer league. Upon his return to England in 1979 he accepted a position with Brighton as Chief Scout. He introduced some very good players to establish an attacking Brighton team and later was appointed team Manager. He was an immediate success and in 1983 he proudly led the Brighton team on to the Wembly turf for the Cup Final against Manchester United.

BOBBY CAMPBELL

Born in Penrhyn Street in 1936. Attended St. Anthony's school and during an outstanding schoolboy career, won many medals. His football talent soon earned him selection for the Liverpool Boys' team and later he won County honours with Lancashire Boys. He represented England at under 18 level.

He joined Liverpool's ground staff in June 1953 and later was captain of the England Youth team which toured Europe. He signed as a professional in 1955 and captained the Liverpool Central League side in season 1956-57. During his National Service he captained the Army team.

He was transferred to Portsmouth in 1961 and captained the team to the Division Three Championship. Later, when his playing career ended, he was appointed Trainer/Coach at Portsmouth. He left the Fratton Park club to become Team Coach at Queens Park Rangers and then coached such talent as Liam Brady and David O'Leary during his period as coach with Arsenal.

He managed Fulham for four seasons and made a very valuable contribution towards erasing a £3/4m debt. He put in a tremendous amount of effort at Craven Cottage and introduced many promising youngsters into the game. He was appointed Manager of Portsmouth in 1982 and in his first full season as Manager, led the club to promotion to Division Two.

LAURIE CARBERRY

Born in Doncaster Street, attended St. Anthony's school. Won many honours during his schoolboy career. In July 1953 he had trials with Everton and played in the Central League team. During his National Service he was stationed at Bury St. Edmunds and played for the Army and the local team. He was spotted by an Ipswich talent scout and later signed professional forms for Ipswich. He